The Daily Miracle

A Memoir of Newspapering

—ɯ—

*"Time is passing my dear
and soon no one will know what you and I know."*

Vladimir Nabokov, "Speak, Memory"

By C. Fraser Smith

Otter Bay Books
BALTIMORE, MD 2019

Please direct all correspondence and book orders to:
Fraser Smith
2600 St. Paul Street
Baltimore, MD 21218

Library of Congress Control Number 2019911283
ISBN 978-1-64633-056-0

Published for the author by
Otter Bay Books, LLC
3507 Newland Road
Baltimore, MD 21218-2513

www.otter-bay-books.com

Printed in the United States of America

This Book is for

**Ruth Bailey,
bff**

CONTENTS

Introduction	....	vii
Prologue	....	xi

Part I

Chapter 1	A Bargain...	1
Chapter 2	Stringing Sentences..............................	5
Chapter 3	"Man in the Street".............................	8
Chapter 4	Instant Memorial.................................	14
Chapter 5	"Write Something"...............................	17
Chapter 6	Newspaper Democracy.........................	23
Chapter 7	The "Joisey"..	30
Chapter 8	Mr. Fixit..	32
Chapter 9	Fashion Plate..	34
Chapter 10	Tribune...	37
Chapter 11	Overtime..	38
Chapter 12	Eddie...	41
Chapter 13	Dog and Pony Show............................	44
Chapter 14	Little Big Man......................................	47
Chapter 15	Thomas Aquinas..................................	51
Chapter 16	The Metallic Mantis............................	53
Chapter 17	A Ridiculous Number..........................	56
Chapter 18	The Bard...	59

Part II

Chapter 19	The Boy Next Door..............................	67
Chapter 20	General Assignment.............................	71
Chapter 21	Jack..	75
Chapter 22	The Role of Women.............................	81
Chapter 23	Are You Neck'st?..................................	86
Chapter 24	Hair Shirt..	90
Chapter 25	Vultures...	93
Chapter 26	Rita..	95
Chapter 27	Hartford Park.......................................	97
Chapter 28	Low-Hanging Fruit..............................	102
Chapter 29	Odd Couple..	106

Chapter 30   Bricks, Soup and a Seat at the Table.............................. 110

Chapter 31   Henry.. 114

Chapter 32   Kangaroo.. 116

Chapter 33   Rockstar.. 120

Chapter 34   Big Plans, Small Minds.. 125

Chapter 35   Watergate and the Rest of Us.. 129

Chapter 36   Kiff.. 131

Part III

Chapter 37   The Newspaper and the City.. 137

Chapter 38   A New Neighborhood.. 138

Chapter 39   Pinnacle... 142

Chapter 40   Nothing Could Be Done with Such Men........................ 147

Chapter 41   Ettlin... 149

Chapter 42   Clown Car.. 152

Chapter 43   The "Hard" Vote.. 157

Chapter 44   With Pulp... 162

Chapter 45   The Mikes... 166

Chapter 46   New Management... 170

Chapter 47   Computers.. 173

Chapter 48   Invasion.. 175

Chapter 49   Reporter's Rules... 180

Chapter 50   Not Even Close.. 183

Chapter 51   Enemy of the People.. 187

Chapter 52   The Memorial... 190

Chapter 53   Sun Lies... 193

Part IV

Chapter 54   Bloody Tuesday.. 198

Chapter 55   Freddy Gray, Invisible Man.. 202

Chapter 56   The Printers' Mass... 207

Chapter 57   And Now?... 210

Chapter 58   The ProJo... 212

Chapter 59   The *Sun*.. 217

Chapter 60   A Grace Note.. 221

Chapter 61   Cigar Box.. 223

Chapter 62   Ring the Bells... 227

Acknowledgments 231

INTRODUCTION

We called it The Daily Miracle. There were so many exacting people doing so many demanding jobs: How in the world did it come out every day? Sometimes we said miracle in a mocking tone, some editor or other having messed with a brilliant lede or cut the best quote. Idiots.

Of course, it wasn't a miracle at all. (And editors weren't idiots.) What readers took to the breakfast table sprang from a remarkable union of hot metal, paper, ink and judgment.

Every day's paper was the result of extraordinary commitment, craftsmanship and experience. Nor did the paper flow from a single day's work. Decades of thinking and re-thinking were behind every page. Each copy was the result of constant efforts to be better – to be perfect, actually. That was the goal. Unlike the car manufacturer that allows a faulty ignition switch to go uncorrected or dismantles a pollution control system, good newspapers printed their errors every day. A culture of perfection shaped them. A state of the city or state or nation arrived at your home, not once a year, but every day: Problems to solve. Priorities to set. Life and death. Stability and change. Without fear or favor. Light for all.

The newspaper, itself, was not immune to change. Nothing new here in the manufacturing life. Weren't the buggy and buggy whip manufacturers eclipsed by change – by the automobile? No big deal. But the buggy and whip had no role in governing – preserving democracy. Newspapers were the backbone of self-government, the oxygen-carrying capillaries of the body politic.

All over the country, whirling behemoth presses produced not just news but the marching orders of daily life: a *Sun*, a *Journal*, a *Mirror* – even a *Picayune* or a *Bee* – each one a marvel if not quite a miracle.

Not every paper, to be sure, measured up to its own or to industry standards. Some allowed owners or political powers to insinuate themselves into the news. A few denied coverage to individuals or causes they did not favor. Editors sometimes served their own interests.

But many or most operated under something like the *Baltimore Sun's* "Light for All" promise. Even the less good papers were valuable, offering sounding boards, a medium of comparison.

In the era of Trump, who calls reporters enemies of the people and purveyors of "fake news," the big three national newspapers have gained strength. The threatening change in tone and style of national leadership drove citizens to the *New York Times*, the *Washington Post* and the *Wall Street Journal*. At the same time, exemplary regional papers – the papers most voters read – fell under the killing pressure of the Internet. The backbone weakened. Many papers went dark. Some survived as shells – ghosts of the enterprise charged with monitoring government and equipping citizens.

The collective news hole (space available for stories) shrank along with the number of reporters and editors, bought out or pushed out. Papers tried to save themselves by PR: We will do more with less, said the hospice managers. They cannot and they know it.

The performance of newspapers in extremis – and many of them are in extremis – has been less than courageous. They mislead the citizenry by pretending to be as good as they once were.

"More with less" is the death rattle. A good regional paper of size and judgment and boldness surely would be a miracle now. Newspaper carcasses litter the landscape, and members of society, I fear, have no clear understanding of what they are losing. A study showed many Americans have no idea that newspapers are dying.

A catastrophic loss unrecognized. Newsrooms, once a marvel of group creativity, give way to bloggers working today in isolation. Those craftsmen who improved, perfected and rejected a writer's work have been dismissed.

We are warned against nostalgia. We must move forward. Yes. But we can and must look back as well. Contrary to movie or TV or novel-drawn images, the newsroom's legacy is intense commitment to the work, fierce devotion to principles of dealing with people fairly, dogged insistence on transparency and the people's right to know.

The irony is that we seldom showed our personal devotion to these standards. We were proudly, devoutly silent about ourselves in an over-hyped world. We trusted readers to know we worked hard to get it right, to find the best available version of the truth – and then to do it all again the next day and the next.

This book chronicles a reporter's half-century, three-newspaper career. It serves also, unavoidably, as a cultural and political history of this country. And perhaps as an obituary.

My newspaper colleagues and I bent eagerly to the goal of perfection, knowing it was a dream. In and out of the newsroom we found kindred souls, men and women committed to grand objectives including support of democracy. They were, in some cases, mirrors. We admired them, marveled at their commitment, saw ourselves in them – introduced them to their neighbors.

The world needed to know what we knew.

PROLOGUE

The glassed-in wire room stood to the left of my gray steel desk with its cut-out, lap-level shelf for a typewriter.

I was new to the newsroom, fascinated by everything. Occasionally when the sound-moderating door to the wire room was open, I could hear one of the teletype machines pulse into action.

They came on and seemed to hover over themselves before settling into a line-by-line, rhythmic transmission. (A wire story "moved" or "landed." I inhaled my new vocabulary).

The wires gave us the world.

They put us on the ground in Washington, D.C., Paris, Beijing, Dallas – anywhere a newspaper had to be.

The machines projected a reassuring hum. We were in the game.

Most of the time, a wire story demanded no immediate action. Sometimes, often, stories rolled out of the machines to pile up in a whorl on the floor. Most of them would never make the paper.

The copy boy attendant, balancing a dozen chores, seemed to know without checking when something important was moving. If there was something useable, he ripped it out of the machine with a muted matador's flair. With less drama, he reeled in the discards.

Any wire story we ran carried the news service name: Associated Press, United Press International, principally. A reporter was out there doing what I thought I might do some day. (If I ever got an assignment.)

Bigger newspapers had their own bureaus across the nation and the world. The *Jersey Journal* where I started with newspapers in 1963, had the wires.

They would bring us coverage of President Kennedy's trip to Dallas. No concern of mine.

The news from a presidential trip, I learned, might begin and end with accounts of his reception. Maybe there would be an obvious angle. How would this part of the South receive him? Would this be the story of a nation moving past the political and religious (anti-Catholic) issues that marked his campaign? Would throngs – or empty spaces – define the mood?

The hearing-acute wire room attendant would be alert .

Sound – the teletypes starting and stopping, the bells signaling the arrival of a story -- defined every step of the process. Bells rang more loudly and longer depending on the story's importance.

"Datelines" along with a one or two-word description topped each story.

The sounds helped me repress the idea of marching up to the city desk with – with what? Occasionally, I just zoned out.

Then I heard the wire room bells ringing and ringing. This was a fifteen-bell alert. It was 12:30 p.m. November 22, 1963.

In a moment, I saw the wire room attendant, already in the room, half-spinning out the door, story in hand, run-walking to the national editor's desk.

One word came before the Dallas dateline:

"URGENT"

A Bargain

As my three-year Air Force career crept to an end, my boss urged me to sign on for the rest of my life. Well, not really, but 20 more years sounded like forever.

Our squadron had just aced one of those snap readiness drills, proving we could move 30 or so fighter planes from our base in northern Japan to various flashpoints in Southeast Asia.

Logistics – moving men and machines from one place to another – was my official Air Force specialty. (There were people who found this fact amusing. Logisticians are life-and-death organized. Me, not so much.)

Somehow my Air Force boss missed my deficiencies. Or, he'd been handed a recruiting quota.

"You're really good at this," he said as we basked in praise from Command.

Nice to hear. But he knew – and I knew – our success owed almost everything to the non-commissioned officers. They were lifers. They knew and did everything. I got the credit. This was the military way. Rank has its privileges even for second lieutenants like me. Anyway, I had no interest in a military career.

Major Bob Minor, my boss... I know, you're thinking 'Major Minor,' real-life Catch 22 craziness.

Not at all. He kept after me.

"Think of all the travel," he said. "See the world on Uncle's dime."

Rapid promotions were almost guaranteed, he said. I knew that was part of the official script, not a guarantee. Why was he still a major, nearing the end of his 20?

He offered what he must have thought was the deal-closer: "You could start a whole new career at age 45 with a nice retirement check."

"You know," I said, realizing I'd have to extricate us both.

"All that sounds great. It's just not for me."

I wanted out. I'd been institutionalized – at university or in the military – long enough.

I wanted to write. Great bits of fiction were not flowing from my brain; so I thought I would write for newspapers. I thought that would be exciting and even useful. I would see some of life. I would improve my writing skills.

I had talked with a retired news guy I knew in Pinehurst, North Carolina, where I grew up. He told me reporters typically got experience and sold it over and over, moving to better and better papers. That was a typical career path, he said. Only problem: I'd have to spend five years in the boondocks learning.

On the long flight back from Japan, I decided to see if I couldn't shorten the process.

A week or so after I got home, I drove to New York. Friends of a friend said they would put me up. They were interested, maybe even impressed, to hear that I was headed for the *New York Times*.

We talked at dinner.

"You're having an interview?" one of them asked.

"Well, I hope so," I said. Then I made a joke about my winning personality and impressive initiative. I knew it was a long shot but I did think I had a shot.

One of the two women glanced at the other. I think they smiled politely.

The next morning, I made my way to Times Square, remarked to myself what a factory-like place a newspaper was right there in the middle of show town – all those trucks and loading docks and noise.

"I'd like to see the editor," I said to the receptionist. I gave her my name.

"Do you have appointment?"

"No," I said.

I think she stifled a sigh. She pressed the No Appointment button on her telephone console.

A minute or so later, a woman in a gray pin-striped business suit came around the corner. A tight bun clung to the back of her head.

She paused a moment.

Then she said: "Mr. Smith?"

I nodded.

"Come with me."

I walked behind her to an office with a window looking out on the brick wall and fire escape of the next building over. Another woman, her assistant I supposed, fell in behind us.

"How can I help?" she asked as we sat down. I might have been in an insurance company office. The woman – Madeleine Worth, according to the wooden name plate on her desk – smiled an abbreviated, official smile.

"I'm looking for a newspaper job," I said.

Her eyes said, "I know."

"What experience do you have," she asked.

"Well, I don't have any experience," I said. "But I would be willing to start as a copy boy."

I was 27 years old, a graduate of the University of North Carolina, well-traveled, an officer and a gentleman by act of Congress (a joke Second Lieutenants made to themselves). I was over six feet tall, reasonably well brought out – curly brown hair still militarily short, shoes shined and ready to start work that day. The U.S. Air Force, the U.S government coveted me, so I figured the *Times* would surely be thrilled to have my very modest self.

True, I had no newspaper experience. But so what? I would learn everything in a month or two. I was sure The Times broke the rules occasionally and hired people who looked like they could overcome a lack of the usual qualifications.

I realized later I must have been talking to the newspaper's Clueless Applicant officer.

Pause.

"When will I be getting to the newsroom?" I asked.

"You won't be," she said. Soft landings were not her way.

Editors were busy. They had no time for people who stumbled in off the street, offering themselves as bargains to the *New York Times*. In fact, I learned later, editors didn't have time for applicants who were qualified. She shifted into hyper explanatory tone.

"A copy kid at the *Times* has five years of reporting experience at a small paper where the inexperienced get a chance to do everything but sell the paper on street corners." A hint of a smile.

She paused.

So, this was not going to be an opportunity for me to prove that rigid adherence to rules could mean loss of talent. Apparently, the *Times* did not think there was much of a risk.

She then handed me off to her assistant, a far less-rule bound person who walked me to the door.

Maybe she saw I had no Plan B.

"I have a friend at a placement firm. She knows an editor at the *Jersey Journal* in Jersey City. Sometimes he has something."

I have no idea why she decided to intervene. I don't think it was the military haircut. Maybe she saw something admirably plucky in my effort. Maybe it was a favor to her friend, a head-hunter of sorts. There would be a fee if I actually got a job in Jersey City. I didn't think about it much at the time. I was way luckier than I had a right to be.

Stringing Sentences

$\mathbf{I}$ called from the first pay phone. (A pay phone was a rectangular closet or coffin-sized, upright room with an accordion-style door for easy access. Often, they were decorated with discarded chewing gum. Some people apparently mistook them for urinals.)

"Come on over," the headhunter said.

I ran the 12 blocks to her office.

She made a call.

"I have a young man…"

She smiled at me, nodding her head "yes" as she got off the phone.

"He says come on over. His name is Gene Farrell."

Among the many things I didn't know then was how to get to Jersey City. She rolled her eyes when I asked for directions.

The newspaper was in Journal Square, just across the river, and across the street from the subway entrance and exit. It didn't occur to me then that having your newspaper's name on the city's central square – the *Times* and Times Square, for example – spoke dramatically to a newspaper's importance in cities. Sure, it was a city, but nothing like New York City or even one of the small North Carolina cities – nothing much other than the newspaper.

I came up the escalator blinking into the sunlight. Off to my right I saw a strikingly ornate movie palace. Nondescript businesses lined the street. Next to these I saw the newspaper entrance.

There were three long flights of stairs to the *Journal* offices. I noticed the composing room off to the left not far from the newsroom. I could hear the machinery, the presses, and see the linotype operators with their green eyeshades. Maybe this would be a place like the one described by the *Times'* anti-initiative lady, a paper where you learned everything.

There was no greeter team. And no waiting. I was in Farrell's office immediately. I gave him a quick bio. He squinted at me over half glasses, graying hair slicked back above ample, dark eyebrows. Occasionally he smiled an agreeable smile, barely parting his thin lips.

"Do you have clips?" he asked. Clips were your best newspaper stories scissored from papers where you had worked.

"No," I said.

"What's your experience then?"

I did my best with this obviously important question. I told him I had written essays for the *Daily Tar Heel*, the University of North Carolina's student newspaper. He didn't ask how many and I didn't volunteer the number (2).

I had planned to try out for a reporter's slot. I had listed it as one of my credits for the Class of 1960 yearbook: "*Daily Tar Heel*, 4" (meaning senior year). I had such high expectations of myself. So well-motivated. But I never got around to presenting myself at the paper.

Thinking more about it later, I remember having been intimidated in the Tar Heel newsroom. All that energy and focus. Everyone seemed to know what they were doing. Where would I fit in? Maybe that's why I didn't try to work there.

Yearbooks came out near the end of senior year so I never had to explain to any of my friends how I had, it seemed, phonied up my credits. I didn't mention any of this to Farrell.

"What makes you think you can do newspaper work?" he asked.

"I'm pretty sure I could string a few sentences together," I said. I think that's just about exactly what I said. I must have sounded a little full of it, essentially dismissing the man's professional life as something I could master overnight. I had little to go on beyond feigned confidence.

Maybe Farrell thought he heard some of the swagger a reporter would need in a place like Jersey City. About all I knew of it then was that its mayor had been the historic boss of political bosses, Frank Hague. He had served eight terms – 30 years – as Jersey City mayor. He seemed to have mastered the art of what some called honest graft.

He demanded a percentage of a city worker's pay. He increased the number of city workers, which kept the money flowing. These kickbacks came on "rice pudding day," when city employees got their pay checks or raises. But most of Hague's big money must have come from his share of public works projects like his famous city hospital, which had the political advantage of being available to city residents, rich or poor. He hired many and could fire them as well. A sharp dresser, he preferred high-neck shirt collars which made him seem more a dandy than a boss. He carried that element of style into his 700-pound, hammered copper coffin.

Hague was elected first as a reformer, with the *Jersey Journal's* help. The relationship soured as Hague's corrupt practices became clear. –

A reporter covering even the vestiges of a corrupt regime would have some learning to do. Or maybe Farrell was always in the market for cheap labor. But nobody was showing me the door.

I was brazening my way through – never my style, though I did think I could manage if I got a chance. Actually, there wasn't much risk for him. I'd be on probation for three months. He could dump me easily enough. Fair warning. I was on my own.

3

"Man in the Street"

Starting a new job of any kind may be like jumping on a moving train. Newspapers? Even more challenging. There was a paper to get out. Not that I would have much to do with it. Fairly quickly, I realized what stories would be coming my way: none at all. Good thing. I didn't know how much I didn't know. My new bosses were flying blind as well. What can this guy do? Whatever, it wasn't going to be needed that day. No time for instruction or do-overs. I would get a press release, a police item – if that. Or an obituary.

I started learning Jersey City funeral home by funeral home. I found a story in every one of them. When I had the obit shift, I got high on the certainty of a story.

Otherwise, I sat in a classroom-like row of general assignment reporters, some as green as I was, waiting. I was excited and eager. But sometimes I daydreamed. Worse than that, I lamented my job interview with Farrell.

"What makes you think you can do this work?" he had asked.

"I think I can manage to string a few sentences together," I had said. I winced every time I re-ran the conversation in my head.

I tried to focus on Semple, Ron Semple, the city editor. Every move. *Maybe Farrell told him what I said.* If Semple got up, all of us in assignment row thought:

"Maybe he's on his way to me." More likely he needed a bathroom break.

I had been at the *Journal* for less than two months. Obviously, I would have no role in covering the president's trip to Dallas. Might not be that exciting anyway. A mostly ceremonial visit. But it was the president of the United States, a president like no other. Star quality we had never seen before in the White House. Kennedy's predecessors arrived via wars or long striving on the ladder of upward political mobility. Kennedy skipped most of that. He moved sharply, gracefully past the usual dues-paying. Gifted with wit, a knowing smile and his father's money, he had charisma, for me a new word for leadership.

Jackie, his aristocratic wife, completed the Texas entourage. People wanted to see a president and his wife. They came out for the show. Even if they didn't agree with his politics or because, in this case, of their religious differences.

The news from such a trip, I would learn, might begin and end with accounts of the president's reception. In this case just arriving carried significance. How would he handle less than adoring citizens? Would this be an opportunity to write about the nation moving past its differences? Would applauding throngs along the motorcade route be evidence of this passage? The high-powered correspondents would find ways to show us what we needed to know.

Reporters would compete with their colleagues for the best "color" story, some element of significance salted in, maybe. A silk purse from a sow's ear, they would say, maybe groaning to themselves at the cliché then new to me.

At 12:30 I heard 15 bells coming from the wire room, then saw the attendant tearing into the newsroom with the story:

"Shots fired at the presidential limousine."

Had anyone been hit? Had the president been hit? Officially, no one knew, UPI reported.

But then, in paragraph three, a quote. The UPI reporter, White House correspondent Merriman Smith, did know.

"He's dead," Smith wrote, quoting a Secret Service agent without naming him. (Later, it would emerge that the agent was Clint Hill, a veteran on the presidential detail.)

The editors in Jersey City and UPI subscribers around the world were looking at each other and saying: "How the hell does he know?"

Soon they would know exactly how.

Hill had jumped onto the rear bumper of the president's convertible limousine. Only a few feet away, he could see Kennedy's catastrophic head wound. Fatal, he knew. He tried to assist Jackie's frantic effort to cradle and shield her husband.

The limousine sped to Parkland Hospital, 12:30 East Coast Time.

Smith met Hill as the agent came out of the hospital emergency room.

The two men knew each other well.

"He's dead, Smitty," Hill said. Smith knew everyone in the Kennedy and before that Eisenhower White House. (Ike had started calling him Smitty).

Beat reporters, reporters covering a single on-going story or office, knew everyone. They knew whose information could be trusted. They knew these things so they would be ready for moments like this. Smith knew he could "go" with Hill's account.

In the *Jersey Journal's* city room, Farrell stood outside his office. Reporters and editors crowded up behind him, waiting for orders.

I thought I heard him say "re-act," with hard emphasis on the first syllable. What he wanted came along with the way he said the word. Semple was literally pushing reporters out the door.

He saw the question on my face.

"Talk to people. Find out what they're thinking."

Short for reaction, re-act was the local response to big news — declarations of war, the election of Popes, the death of a Babe Ruth-caliber sports star.

This is what local newspapers did. the *New York Times* or the *Washington Post* or the *Wall Street Journal*, the wires, they would have the big story. The major papers would interview regular people, too, but for papers like the *Jersey Journal,* "man in the street" was to be the story.

As we ran down three flights of stairs to the street and left the building, all we knew was "shots fired." We hadn't had time to read the UPI story.

"Shots fired"? Big story, dead or alive.

Agent Hill was right. The president was dead – officially declared so – at 1 p.m. Central Time. A newspaper or wire service would want an official source before reporting a death, particularly in a case like this. UPI had trusted Smith. Like every wire service, UPI wanted to be first.

Wire service lore marveled later at Smith's near ownership of the story. He'd been the lead "pool" reporter, the one in the press car closest to the president. Smith had the only available phone in these pre-cellular days. He refused to give it up, causing the Associated Press reporter to pummel him on the way to the hospital. Smith prevailed. Nothing fair about it, but no one seemed to fault him for it. I learned all this much later.

The world leapt into a dizzying dimension of time. Life changed in a jarring fraction of a second. This man we hardly knew, though closer to us than any other president, was dead? For many of us, this level of vulnerability had no precedent.

People on the street knew before we did. The live story featuring Hill was all over TV, that revolutionizing medium just then moving into the center of life. Commuters coming up escalators from the Hudson tube from lower Manhattan to Jersey City could see and hear the story through restaurant and bar windows.

Women in a beauty parlor watched the CBS television anchor Walter Cronkite struggle to steady his voice as he announced Kennedy's death.

People reacted as Cronkite had -- with shock, fear, confusion, anger and instant theories of who did the shooting, even a bit of scolding.

"How could he be driving down there in an open car?" And another leap to ID the shooter. Or shooters:

It was Communists. Or Baptists or Catholicism haters.

Frank Baran, unaware of the events in Dallas, complained about the crowds.

"Maybe the president's been shot," he said to his wife. You could joke about something you thought would never happen. Brought up to speed, Baran sagged against his wife's shoulder.

"Did he die? My God!" Margaret Snellingove of Bergenfield, said, "I heard it while I was eating lunch. I got sick."

A policeman standing alone sobbed.

We were working individually, talking with anyone who would stop. One or two of the people I spoke with wondered if the unthinkable was actually less than surprising.

"It was always an apprehension," said Harry Forbes of Jersey City. "The percentages seemed to be in favor of something like this."

Some blamed Kennedy.

"Just what you're asking for when you run for president," said a man who wanted his name withheld.

"This country is full of imbeciles," said Mrs. Maryanna Donahue.

"I feel disgraced," said Mrs. Josephine Castorama, a ticket sales lady at Loews Theater on Journal Square.

You were hearing not only what people thought about the shooting or murder of a President but tracings of their views about life and politics and their country.

Insight or artful turns of phrase would have been welcome, but you had a workaday objective: You were making men and women readers part of the story. You were collecting voices and emotions for a human mosaic of anguish and sadness and fear.

The hometown newspaper said, *It matters what you think*. The exercise was a trope, something newspapers did. What had people thought at FDR's passing – or a vital young president mortally wounded in Texas?

Our team turned out to be good at this. Few if any of us had done anything like it before -- not on this scale.

No smart, incisive questions were needed. Good thing. I was as rattled as the people I stopped. Probably helped me. They could see it.

"You know what's happened," I said. "Tell me your thoughts." For me then, doubly concerned – about my country and my job -- stopping people at moments like this seemed intrusive, even rude. I felt guilty. I knew I couldn't have offered any coherent thoughts of my own. I felt as if a chasm had opened in front me. Could I keep my balance? Would I be sucked down by some force unfelt by me before then?

In short order on November 22, the newspaper had the first of five "EXTRA" editions on the street. The headline on the first of these:

"JFK SHOT! DYING?"

Events were outpacing the presses. Next came the official declaration of the president's death at Parkland Memorial Hospital. Then place names and other details of this still-resonating moment in history – Dealey Plaza, where the president was ambushed; the Texas School Book Depository from which the shots were fired; and the Zapruder film, named for the man who found himself recording the story of a century; Agent Hill on the back of the limousine. These became bits of American history as well-known as Washington's cherry tree.

In Extra #5, *The Jersey Journal's* banner read:

"JFK ASSASSINATED!"

"What is assassinated?" asked a young boy out shopping with his mother. "It means murdered," said a woman who overheard the question.

Death or impending death often comes to us slowly. We see it coming. We pray to stop it or slow its advance. This death denied us any preparation. The President of the United States assassinated? Had it really happened? Many knew presidents had been murdered, of course. Kennedy was the fourth. But in books, in history, to figures we had never seen alive. To bearded old men. Not to vibrant, handsome young ones. And yet, because he was the first Catholic president, there had been more than the usual concern. Worry was the handmaiden of premonition.

The world had changed. But who could say how?

I felt dislocated from my surroundings, a profound dizziness. But I was asking others to express themselves. As in every newspaper story, the reporter is also a citizen, but professionalism demands a separation. With time, I would achieve more of it.

4

Instant Memorial

I composed my paper, picking from the clips and cables and filed copy, the world picture I would invent for my readers...

E.L. Doctorow, "The Waterworks"

Invent? Sort of.

Editors invented or created or shaped their product every day, using the sources Doctorow lists. And others he does not: the editor's own knowledge, his experience and judgment. Editors were serial inventors, putting together the best version of their world day after day. Their job included spotting the fake and false and the self-serving. They knew it when they saw it. That brutal, ugly spike on the desk was there for a reason. (Computers came with a digital spike.)

Later in the afternoon, I went into the street a second time, accompanied by a photographer. We needed art (photos) as well as "react." We headed for the subway station just across the street. The lensman had a woman pretend to cry as she held a transistor radio (one of the first handheld devices, circa 1960) to her ear as if waiting for news from the hospital.

"Grief outside the Hudson Tube": Was that the headline idea? We walked back to the newsroom with our photo. I noticed that Farrell seemed slightly annoyed most of the time anyway but this work seemed to offend him.

"Posed?" he asked -- and answered.

He looked at me and the photographer as if to say, "Who thought this was any good?" The photographer had been on the staff for years. I assumed he knew what Farrell would want.

Newspaper photographs in those days were often static, usually shots of people standing still: The cameras and the printing capabilities were not good enough for action shots. Photos were often award shots taken at some civic club, smiling, cheese-mouthing people arranged by the photographer. The prints were made and then shaded or accented or outlined to make the printed versions clearer. Newspapers were just then giving photographs any real attention.

Editor Farrell stifled a groan when he saw the print. The mourner had been caught in a histrionic demonstration of sadness, of hoping for good news but not expecting it. The shot had playacting written all over it.

Farrell didn't linger over his displeasure. Within minutes we were back on the street with a different assignment. More react, certainly, but asking people to think about changing the name of Hudson Boulevard, the county's historic main artery, to John F. Kennedy Boulevard. What did Jersey City, as represented by the men and women we found out and about in this moment of shock and fear, what did they think of this proposal – Farrell's proposal? The dead President's plane might still be in Dallas and we at the *Jersey Journal* were changing street names.

Didn't actually matter what people thought.

"No negative responses," Farrell said as we headed out the door.

It only mattered what *Farrell* thought. The newspaper would pretend to care about what those men and women in the street were thinking because it was the *Jersey Journal,* their newspaper. We wanted to show readers they were important – or, I thought later, that their paper was important. We could be forgiven, I suppose. Here was the most dramatic opportunity any newspaper would ever have to bond with readers. We offered the 10 or 12 men and women we met a role.

But, in the matter of a memorial, we stacked the deck. I learned later, this was the popular assumption: Newspapers made stuff up, shaped and massaged and tailored – invented even as Doctorow slyly put it – all the time. But the papers I worked for over the next many years never did that. We ran what the men and women in the street said – not at length to be sure – but not canted one way or the other. The negative as well as the positive responses ran. On this day, the *Jersey Journal* would tell its readers only what a random sampling of their fellow citizens thought about the president's wounding and death, as long as it agreed with what Farrell thought. He had done it, I decided later, to get ahead of the competition of which there was, in those days, a lot in nearby New York City and in Hudson County, where the *Journal* circulated. You had to give people a reason to buy your paper and not someone else's paper. He probably knew that many other places in the nation would be re-naming streets. He and his city would be one of the first.

In his mind, I suppose, he had moved beyond worrying that orders like this were a slippery slope, a pathway to egregious re-shaping of stories. In this case, the orders seemed wholly unnecessary. People would have agreed to almost any memorial in that atmosphere of desolation and loss. I don't remember finding a single opponent of Farrell's idea.

I never encountered another instance of editorial thumbs on the scale. Had there been anything like it in later years, many of us would have refused – and loudly – if an editor called for such manipulation. A growing sense of power in the newsroom – along with the growing strength of our unions – made us stronger.

5

"Write Something"

From the tube bars or in conversation with re-write as I filed my notes by phone, I learned there would be a national wake in Washington. The president's body would lie in state at the Capitol. The next day, on my own with no assignment, I got on a train for D.C. I was too "new" to be sent on any out of town story. In later years at two other papers, dispatching a reporter would have been automatic. I have wondered if the *Journal* just didn't have the financial resources. If that were the case, sending someone wouldn't have occurred to Semple or Farrell.

I didn't go as a reporter. I went as Colin Fraser Smith, citizen. How could I not? I knew him or felt like I did. TV made us all a part of the drama. At the same time a TV vigil would not be enough. I had to be there. It was a three-hour train ride. I'd be with other frightened, confused people. Maybe that would help me get a handle on things.

During the ride, a slideshow of images flickered through my head. Kennedy's inauguration, his angular face turned a bit to his right, his breath visible; Robert Frost, seeming disoriented as he stood to read the inaugural poem. Later I learned Frost had been blinded by the sun and then, stymied by a balky teleprompter. Was he a bit dotty?

Quite the opposite. Swift enough of mind at 87, he simply recited another of his poems, "The Gift Outright," one he'd long since memorized. It was a better effort I thought than "Dedication," the poem written for Kennedy. "Dedication" was rambling -- unfocused, not particularly lyrical -- seemingly dashed off on deadline. Its last words, though, were piercing:

JFK's election, Frost wrote, came with a promise:

> ... *A golden age of poetry and power*
> *Of which this noonday's the beginning hour.*

Not even an hour. Had all the Kennedy promise died in Dallas?

The whole nation was learning or re-learning how to deal with loss and change in an instant. Some of us leaned against the idea that coping and grieving would end, that time would heal. Yes and no. It was about loss. Some wounds are forever.

Kennedy's election had promised a new beginning. He was no abstract, remote figure. We knew of PT 109, his heroic swim to save his buddies, his book *Profiles in Courage*, all a part of our internalized portrait. He stood there in our mind's eye smiling a bit impishly. He seemed on occasion to be saying, "You didn't think I could do it." And now he was history. It occurred to me later that assassination deprived us in many important ways. There would be no death watch, no time to absorb the looming unimaginable, no time to pray for recovery. We could pray for ourselves and the nation. Could LBJ replace JFK? Get used to it.

I described the weekend to my reporter friends in the newsroom on Monday morning. Semple overheard.

"You ought to write something," he said.

Write something? For the newspaper?

"You wanted an assignment, right? I said to myself.

"Sure, but...

"But what?"

The idea should have occurred to me. I suppose. It had not. I had made myself a participant in the great sadness. But I had never written anything more for the newspaper than an obituary or a "short" or a little feature about the last 15-cent haircut or the re-opening of a synagogue. And now it was thought I might write something about the death of a president?

And there was this added complication. Semple had seemed to me a cartoon character. He had a rounded, enviably thick mustache that covered much of his mouth. He loved pistachio nuts, ate them in the newsroom. They disappeared into the rounded, reddish foliage, with him chewing as he spoke. You couldn't see his lips or his teeth.

It made his orders seem less than authoritative. Whatever. Big opportunity. If I could just string a few sentences together. Right.

And then, suddenly, exhaustion. I'd been standing in a line of mourners for hours and then a wakeful trip back, still battered by what had happened.

But here's the main thing, the thing that made Semple's opportunity so daunting, an odd disjuncture. I'd been living the previous 24 hours outside my job, way outside. Job and life were still separate and distinct for me. I went to Washington as a private citizen, not as a reporter. I was just a mourner. I didn't take a single note or talk to a single person.

I did my best. I wrote what I remembered. I wrote in first person, a rare thing for reporters in the still hyper-objective world then dominant in news writing. (I believe my recollection of this event and my rendering of it here are pretty accurate. My recall, etched into my psyche, has endured. Emotion and fear and heartbreak left little room for art or the kind of discipline I would manage later. I can almost summon the evening air, the flickering lights in the houses we passed on the walk. I am surely not alone in this vivid recalling.)

A National Wake

I stood in a line of grieving people that ended, by the time I got to Union Station in Washington, at Lincoln Park several miles east of the Capitol. There were thousands of us. We walked slowly and, for the most part, silently for the next five hours, moving through the Hill neighborhood's dark, flag and already crepe-shrouded houses. A few people came out of their front doors and onto the sidewalk to join us.

We reached the Capitol grounds about 6:30 a.m. The sun rose behind us. We climbed the sweeping expanse of white marble steps. The reality of what had happened still there to be measured and absorbed. Had a President of the United States really been assassinated? It must be so. We were all there for part of a wake, weren't we? I looked around the grounds still wrapped in dark shadows, hoping for some orientation, some image that might anchor me in the moment. Where had Kennedy taken the oath? Where had Frost tried to read his poem? Oh, yes, it was on the West Front of the building, a vibrant, exciting lifetime away from that morning with its message of death and loss now confronting us.

And then there was a brief moment of communion with a flag-covered coffin. I had been to a funeral home when my father died at 52 and later when a friend from high school was killed in a car crash. But I had not often gone to wakes or memorial services in the small North Carolina town where I grew up.

I had no sense of how people acted at such public events of public mourning – certainly not when the deceased was a president. Who had? All of this was so far from any American's concept of life and death.

I had gone because I thought I should go as an American who could get there with ease. I liked the idea of representing people. It was one of the reasons I wanted to write for newspapers.

The casket stood in the center of the grand Capitol Rotunda. An honor guard, its members representing the various armed forces, was as lifeless-seeming as the body it guarded. They stood at attention, rifles pointed toward the great dome. There was an unnerving stillness. Against my growing acceptance of what had happened, I kept expecting some movement. There was nothing. A shocking, silent solemnity. There was no easing the reality. Presidents die too.

The people walked by slowly, passing within a car's length of a promise that could not be kept. This was not a movie, not a play, not some artfully painful bit of fiction. There was sobbing, heart-crossing, blown kisses.

And then we were gone each in turn, passing back into a damaged world.
The bright morning seemed a rebuke to personal anguish.

I typed "30," newspaper language for The End, a signal to the editor that there was nothing more to come.

I carried the story to the city desk. Semple read it quickly.

He looked up.

"Where are the people?"

I didn't answer.

"You did talk to people, didn't you?" he said.

"No," I said.

"Nobody?"

"No."

"You were out there for five hours and you didn't talk to anyone? What the hell were you doing?"

I didn't want to say interviewing seemed intrusive and inappropriate. Has to be on the hardboiled side, I thought. And then I said, "I didn't think I was working."

"Of course, you were working," Semple said. "You're always working."

My story didn't run. Of course, I have regretted losing a record of that moment, that opportunity to have my name on such an epic story. Then again maybe I hadn't missed anything. Bylines were scarce in those days – and non-existent for reporters as green as I was. And I had simply failed to do the job as Semple envisioned it.

An experienced (or journalism-schooled reporter) would have gotten some extended "react," some interviews. Years later, in a similar story, my piece would have run, I think. Papers would be learning that readers welcomed such stories. Being there got to be much more important. That would have mattered at such a moment. I was the *Jersey Journal's* man. I would have represented a perfect second day local story.

Semple had not sent me to D.C., so maybe the fact that I went there on my own embarrassed him. Why hadn't he sent someone? In my experience, newspapers send reporters to cover many breaking news events or to "work" stories they had discovered elsewhere. The coverage area grew with television and a broader definition of "local." A good story, not merely the home circulation area, became the criterion.

Semple may have been wrong not to send a reporter, but he was right about one thing: From that day forward, I was always working, always thinking about the story I was working on, always thinking about how to get it and how to write it.

6

Newspaper Democracy

The death of a president was not just another death, of course. But in a sense it was. Death and life would go on. And, in Jersey City, I would be in charge of death's immediate public accounting. I would be in charge of lives lived. I wrote obituaries once or twice a week. Purgatory for some reporters. I loved it.

The shift started at 4:30 a.m. Rolled-up duplicates of paid death notices printed on flimsy yellow paper flew at me encased in clear plexi-glass tubes. The last tracings of a life were fitted into these foot-long conveyances. They announced themselves with a drawn-out hiss and thump as the tube landed in a leather-lined, padded box to the right of my desk. A strap pulled over a metal nub kept the spent lives in the tube as it was sucked through the pneumatic pipes, a system of suction that allowed messages to travel to and from all departments of the building without benefit of a human messenger: this was, of course, years before email, years before the net. Pneumatic tubes were about as high tech as it got in those days.

I was to write a story about each of the folded lives. No gunshots were heard. No poets read. No books commissioned. No pomp and circumstance. And yet ... we would celebrate the life, the community, the parents and friends as if the deceased were entitled to this much respect at least.

My colleagues on obits, all older than I, assured me I could call the deceased's family as early as 5 a.m. Pretty self-serving of the newspaper. Even rude. (I was still working through the citizen/reporter separation.) But no, not a disruption at all, I was assured by a colleague with a bit more experience. My call might come at the worst possible moment in someone's life. But grieving people do not sleep well or at all. They're up. My call would be a welcome distraction. People would seize the opportunity to memorialize. A family or its designated representative had the privilege of saying: This was a good person, a kind and generous and accomplished person.

Honors could be enumerated if there were honors. No honors, no problem. For the people of Jersey City, the obit was almost as official as a certificate from the coroner: You lived, you died and *the Journal* recorded your passing.

In some communities, getting ready for the obituary writer was a reflex. You gathered the photographs, the award plaques, the citations, the clippings. The moment lent, when you thought about it, a reassuring and affirming rhythm. The obituary gave the newspaper real status in the life of a community.

The obituary beat was a perfect introduction to a city and to "the business" — to the work I wanted to do. At first, I tried to write something different for each death. I thought some variation would prevent boredom. It seemed demeaning somehow to write the same thing over and over. I produced six or seven of these gems before a copy editor came rushing to my desk.

"Write them all the same," he said, shaking his head.

"Really?"

"Yes, the same." (I was on a steep learning curve. I hoped I would not provoke panic at every turn.)

At the *Jersey Journal* and most other papers, you could say the three-paragraph ritual was democratic. Everyone got their three, no more, no less in most cases.

Unless there was a photograph. That made the deceased a candidate for a kind of posthumous stardom known at the *Journal* as the Feature Obituary. (Later, when I worked for the *Baltimore Sun*, these pieces were called the Mort Du Jour. One of the obit writers there had the perfect name: Dewitt Bliss.) For me and other authors of such pieces, a photograph meant an opportunity to write. There were, of course, no cell phones or the first indications of a camera in every house. Often, then, few people were good at using what they owned in the way of photographic equipment.

One day, with a version of obituary grail in hand, I raced up the stairs from Journal Square to the newsroom. I had a photograph of the late Frank Guggliotta in one hand, my notes in the other. I tried not to be noticeably out of breath as I walked into the newsroom. What I had might have seemed unremarkable to the old heads. My rookie friends – Bob Pearlman, Norma Jehring and Ozzie Johnston – as green as I was, understood.

The photograph meant my story would run prominently— in other words, stripped across the top of the obit page. There was no doubt about "the play" -- where the story would appear, because I had the *sine qua non*, a photo. Officially, you had to have art – aka photograph. No art, no feature.

The objective: along with the picture, 44 lines of type, no more, no less. You got a feel for length as your story rolled through the typewriter.

Forty-four lines became the parameters of a successful life for purposes of the *Jersey Journal's* obituary page. You hoped to find someone at least a little interesting every day. But interesting was less important than the photo. Some of the "art" we found was distinctly marginal. One of my writing gems featured a gentleman who looked as if he had drowned and been photographed on the beach in his final earthly costume, a washed out Hawaiian shirt.

One of those whose life and death I recorded had tended her roses lovingly, cared for her grandchildren, and made a fine chocolate cake. In her photograph, she looked a little like the woman in American Gothic. All the better.

Frank Guggliotta's parents, bless them, provided a head shot of him, smiling in his Army uniform, dark jacket and tan necktie, accented in the shadowy photo.

This was not war reporting. But I was coming back to the newsroom with the equivalent of an Ernie Pyle tone poem from the front. With Frank Guggliotta, I was meeting the requirements – proving myself to myself – as well as to the editors. I was delivering on deadline.

It was not a perfectly equalizing facet of the newspaper's work but finding the elements of life in these stories was driven by a belief that every life we wrote about deserved care and best effort. There were no extra editions for Frank Guggliotta, but I told the story of his life with the same care we had shown with the death of a President.

Like Kennedy, Gugliotta was a veteran. The president lost a brother during the Second World War. Frank lost a friend he'd grown up with. Whose death meant the most? Depended on who you asked.

A Founder of Vets' Club in Memory of Buddy

Members of the Robert E. "Mitch" Kennedy 38th Street Veteran's Club in Union City assembled yesterday to pay last respects to one of the club's founders.

Frank Guggliotta was killed in an automobile accident Tuesday on the New Jersey Turnpike near Burlington. He lived with his parents at 314 37th Street, Union City.

Mr. Guggliotta was one of nine Union City men who enlisted together in 1940 with the National Guard. They were assigned to the 212 Coast Guard Artillery in New York City, and sent to Camp Steward, Ga., One week before they would have been released under their one-year service contract, the Japanese hit Pearl Harbor and the nine started further, intensive training.

They were together for almost two years, transferring to bases in Seattle, Wash., and Newport News, Va., before being separated and sent to European and Pacific theaters.

Frank Guggliotta was one of those who hit the Normandy Beach on D-Day. He was awarded the Purple Heart for injuries he received in Belgium. And he fought in the Battle of the Bulge,

After being listed as missing in action, he was found months later in an English hospital. He came home soon after and spent some time in a Long Island Veterans Hospital recuperating from his wounds.

Robert E. Kennedy was the only one of the nine who did not return. His buddies, who are now living in New Jersey, New York and California decided to start a club in his memory.

They picked the 38th Street location because it was near the site of the old Famous Restaurant, starting point for their activities before the war.

"We met George Schlem, a former Union City cop in the restaurant," John Murphy one of the original nine recalled. He explained that Schlem was a member of the National Guard outfit in New York City and they joined "as one" at his behest.

Most of the nine went to Washington School and to Union Hill High School, Murphy recalls, although he attended Jefferson.

Mr. Guggliotta was a pipefitter's assistant and he belonged to the Pipefitter's Union, Local 274. He was also a member of the Union City Regular Organization Democratic Club.

Mr. Guggliotta is survived by his mother and father, Mr. and Mrs. Blaise Guggliotta; five brothers, John, Joseph, Anthony, Dominick and William; and two sisters, Mrs. Florence Mass and Mrs. Mary Pasante.

The funeral will be today from the Clerici Funeral Home in Jersey City with a mass at St. Rocco's.

I was eager to move on, to handle more "substantive" assignments. But I realized that nothing was more substantive than stories like Frank's. In most of the obituaries I wrote, there was more than the story of one man's life. It was the story of a city, a story of friendship and of war, of suggestions that seemed fateful eventually, ill fortune and virtual resurrection.

Frank's family would let his buddies know if they hadn't seen the accident story in the *Journal*. But the newspaper (and I) would get the news to the man's barber, the waitress he kidded at the coffee shop, the dry-cleaning clerk who knew he wanted light starch in his shirts, his friends at St. Rocco's. He would not be stopping by on his errands. He would not be there for a quick one after work.

And what of the woman who walked an evergreen wreath around her church every year on All Saints Day, asking the faithful to make a contribution: a dollar bill pinned to the wreath was the usual tribute. She had started doing this after she thought prayers for a seriously ill son had been answered. She would not forget her promise.

The fully subscribed All Saints Day garland was laid at Our Lady's Altar in Our Lady of Mt. Carmel church. This gesture of faith in God and community was what the woman, Mary Verdiramo, lived for, her purpose in life.

In a story like this, I thought, the newspaper introduced us to each other. Where did others find meaning in life? The newspaper offered us perspective unavailable otherwise. We might not have recognized its lesson. It made us part of a community, gave us a way to see beyond our own likes and dislikes and beliefs.

And there was more to this story. What Mrs. Verdiramo wanted most in life, she told her son, Vincent, was to die on All Saints Day. And she did. Was this the power of will? Of prayer? Had the divine intervened? Who knew? But it happened and the *Jersey Journal* recorded it.

It came under the heading of "amazing news" – laughed at a little but treasured. Some editors called a story like this "a slice of life," a cliché that seemed to cheapen something remarkable. The slice seemed to balance perfectly on the line between hope and belief. And it was more than a slice. It was life itself.

Over the next many years, media wanted more and more stories of personal lives – particularly if death had come during wartime or after a terrorist attack – a World Trade Center bombing, the bombing of Marine barracks in Beirut, a mass shooting at a high school or a movie theater. Schooled first by newspapers and then by television, people saw the obituary as the defining endpoint. In recent years, people developed – or media implanted a need – for public mourning. People started to await the obituary writer's call – or a team from the TVs. It was more therapeutic than I realized when I was doing it. It got more so. Technology had introduced real cultural change, new public rituals, maybe even more balm and succor.

The chase made some of my colleagues impatient. And sometimes their efforts were hilarious, or calamitous.

My friend Pearlman, who had worked for a CARE-like organization before deciding to try newspapers, found a feature obit one day in the account of a crane operator killed on the job.

"Bill McEnerney always said he wanted to die in the saddle and that's exactly what happened yesterday," he wrote. The story went on to describe the accident on a building site.

Semple read the lead and jumped from his chair. We saw him coming toward us.

"Are you aware," he asked Pearlman, "of the pejorative meaning of the phrase 'die in the saddle'?" Norma Jehring, another relatively new but very sharp and mature new reporter, turned away. I waited to hear Semple describe the desire to die while lovemaking.

"I didn't know," Pearlman said.

Semple headed back to the city desk.

Pearlman and Norma and I stood in a long line of young reporters who did this work. We learned about our city. We learned the immutable obituary formula and why it was immutable – even-handedness. We learned how to write profiles, a newspaper staple.

One of our predecessors, Eugene Flinn, had gone on to teach journalism at a local university. He was the premier writer of the obit genre, a practitioner of legendary skills. They called him Formaldehyde Flynn.

"You won't be here long enough to be that good," I was told by the night editor.

What did that mean? I decided to take it as a compliment. He had told me earlier I had "handled" a story well. Handled. I liked the verb. I liked the sound and feel of a word that suggested some skillful organization of material, some felicitously quick and economical recounting of a person's life, maybe even a resonating theme. It made me feel like I could actually do what I assured Farrell I could do. Maybe it meant I had some talent. Only my limited longevity in the job stood in the way. Otherwise, I told myself, I *could* be as good as Flinn.

7

The "Joisey"

A conversation overheard in Jersey City:

"You know the flu killed more people than bombs during World War I."

"Really? How do you know?"

"I read it in da Joisey."

The *Jersey Journal*, referred to then and now as "da Joisey," was the go-to source. (Google, etc., not yet available.) The newspaper had been as much a part of their lives as daily milk delivery or dad asleep in the Barcalounger after a Manhattan and another day of work at the electric company. The newspaper had been at the center of city life for decades. The city's business hub, Journal Square, was named for it. Five-foot high red letters stood on top of the newspaper's building. Its daily presence, if not the news it brought, was something to rely on. It landed on the front porch or in the shrubbery or pulled from the boxes outside the Hudson Tube station every day. It was part of life's rhythm. Many readers, thinking nothing of it, had adopted their newspaper, given it a nickname, a shorthand understood by all.

Smart-ass reporters, including me, repeated what we heard on the street. We were mocking the accent, partly. But also the thought of anyone taking what a newspaper reported as gospel. We had arrived in the newsroom with our own version of the stereotypes everybody else had: newspapers were "rags," you wrapped the fish in them; they were written for 8th graders; not true by the way. And on and on. We were missing something big.

"Don't believe everything you read in the newspaper," people said in Jersey City and anywhere newspapers were printed. No, and most of the

Joisey's readers did not. But the newspaper was the starting point. It was accorded that much trust automatically. And it was quite a bit of trust. What the newspaper reported were the talking points of a citizenry.

The daily reports came close to a tangible frame for life in the city. Sports, city hall, the courts, the arts, bake sales, church notices, the volunteer fire department's ham and bean supper, obituaries, the numbers: Life. The newspaper didn't call itself a journal for nothing. It was a daily account of life in the neighborhoods, on the theater screens, in corporate boardrooms. If anything of note had happened over the previous 24 hours, only a few individuals knew until the paper arrived. The state of the city was there in da Joisey and nowhere else.

"I read it in da Joisey," I realized later, was a tribute. It wasn't full-on, unquestioning trust, more like accepting until further information was available. If there was nothing further, da Joisey was not just the first draft of history but maybe the last or penultimate. That was, in a way, its reason for being. The high-flown generalities (like this one) were hardly ever mentioned. And in time the paper's authority was there to be rejected or applauded. Who else was keeping track of Jersey City or Hudson County or the state of New Jersey? Only the newspaper. No wonder Farrell thought of himself as master of the universe. He could name streets for fallen presidents, travel to Italy with mayors, keep stories out of his paper and go into movies free. He was the Walter Cronkite of Jersey City. He wasn't saying "And that's the way it is," the way Cronkite did. Not exactly. But he wrote the editorials. He felt perfectly comfortable telling people they should tax themselves more heavily via multi-million-dollar bond issues. No one was going to vote him out of office. They could write letters to the editor. He could print them – or not. It didn't matter within bounds. He was still buying ink by the barrel.

I found some of his performance unsettling. My concerns would grow.

8

Mr. Fixit

Turned out Farrell had something in mind for me. In addition to obituaries, I was to be "Mr. Fixit," a columnist of sorts. The prior person who had done the job for some years, gave me the drill.

People will call or write with questions and problems.

"Your job is to answer quickly and accurately," he said.

Often, I was handling questions like how many miles is it to the moon? Who were the members of the U.S. Supreme Court? What is the electoral college?

"Kids will write in for help with their term papers," Harold said. There was of course no Google, no Wikipedia. I would be a one-man Net for young scholars. Many of these Journal-driven fixes turned into stories. Mr. FIXIT would be a reporter.

One letter writer had this question: "Across the street from my property are a broken-up car, bed mattresses, living room furniture which was dumped over a year ago. This is an eyesore. Do I have to look at this – plus children playing in broken glass and starting fires every so often?"

I wrote, "MR. FIXIT referred your complaint to Nunzio D'Elia, deputy director of public works. D'Elia says the lot has since been inspected and will be cleaned as soon as possible." I was a reporter! I was making something happen! I was intervening on behalf of troubled citizens! I was wielding the power of the press!

After his briefing, Harold stood beside me for a minute.

"Like to see my kidney stones?" he asked. He reached into a desk drawer, pulling out a jar with a dark mass at the bottom. He gave it a shake. A lot of stones. Sounded like a New Year's Eve noisemaker.

I didn't say anything.

"Okay," he said. He put the jar back in the drawer.

There were characters in the Air Force, too. I had gotten to know a few of the pilots on the base in northern Japan, the island of Honshu.

The F-100s they flew were called "lead sleds," planes with no measurable glide path. Without thrust, the plane nosed over and fell out of the sky. If the engine flamed out (stopped running), as they occasionally did, you could try for an "air start." Air flowing rapidly through the engine might get it going again. If not, the flier would have to bail out. Just the struggle to get out -- or get ejected -- sounded pretty hairy. But these guys were into risk. While out on training missions, they occasionally flew under power lines, cutting them with the plane's tail. Japanese government and power company executives were not amused.

Not surprisingly, pilots were heroic drinkers. The brass had considerable tolerance for their cable-cutting pranks. Now and then one of the planes didn't come back.

I wasn't part of this fraternity but in a way, as the person in charge of supplies and logistics, it was dependent on me. Along with the sergeants, I was all over the Far East making sure remote operating bases in South Korea, Thailand, the Philippines had all the necessary equipment to keep the planes flying if we were deployed there. We held periodic, surprise readiness tests.

And now I would be corresponding with high school kids. Not exactly what I'd had in mind. But I was doing it for a newspaper.

9

Fashion Plate

I took one journalism course at UNC. The professor presented himself on the first day of class in chalk-striped gray pants, plaid jacket and yellow shirt with suspenders and a bow tie. He seemed to have thought carefully about how to be in character – as if it were incumbent on him as an experienced scribe to look like a real newspaperman (as seen in the movies).

But a lot was changing in the world of the hack (a reporter's word for reporter). My best newspaper friends came from Harvard and Yale and Princeton and the University of North Carolina. That they were coming from universities at all was change. Or at least a perceived change from the days when reporters were thought to have little if any higher education.

We had no collective motivation. Nothing like the Woodward and Bernstein example drove us to newsrooms. We had no illusions about making history. But, soon enough there it was. We went with a rising tide of news, cultural and social change – all of which would be in our working lives --- or lives in general. We would be, as Semple said, "always working." Wars and war protest, civil rights, the romance of Washington, a less-restrictive reporting role that demanded the kind of broadening some of us were encouraged to get and any number of other compelling stories would become our professional and personal lives.

Kennedy's death, a kind of 100-year event, looks in retrospect like a perfect introduction to the world I would be covering for more than 50 years. More assassinations would follow: in a Los Angeles hotel kitchen – Kennedy's brother, Robert; in a Memphis motel – the Rev. Martin Luther King Jr.; and around the world. A march on the Pentagon. Upheavals in cities across the nation as black people marched for equal justice. Tom Wolfe charged newspaper journalism with hiding the truth behind various conventions and rules. My Kennedy story would have run under Wolfe's rules.

He urged getting to the heart and essence of an issue or player in the public drama. The most controversial aspect of his credo was the use of literary techniques. Worked for magazine writing I thought, not for the daily paper. Simply not enough time or space to write the penetrating profile, the kind that made the reader "experience," rather than simply reading descriptions of people or actions. Over time though, his arguments became the new standards – especially in so-called long-form stories. (This happened, as it turned out, just before newspapers shriveled into a half or a third of their size.)

The news of our era, beginning in my life with JFK's death, threatened the stability in the world. All of us would be breaking new ground. The old guard editors would be holding us in check – or thought they would be. They knew things were changing and they were, in a sense, captive of those who were, me included, productive.

"You know," said my reporter friend Irwin Becker, "you're doing just what they say we can't do." Advocating, he meant.

I didn't see it that way. I was just reporting what I saw -- bureaucratic dishonesty, a failure to act in good faith when the real advocates found unfairness. Recipients and their organizers were finding benefits hidden in the law: Something as banal seeming as "kitchen sets" were among these. Suddenly the welfare bureaucracy was over-spending its budget. So they stopped providing the sets – until the National Welfare Rights Organization charged them with violating the law. I "got away with" advocating, I think, because I was reporting what the advocates were finding. The law offered various goods and services, sometimes buried in the regulations, but denied until the denials were called out. The arrival of well-trained lawyers and other advocates were arming the poor, giving them ammunition. In truth, I would have owned the "advocating" charge. Actually, I was just reporting truths obscured or hidden until the real advocates uncovered them.

If there was advocacy, it gained legitimacy as the newspapers' role in society: advocating fairness and justice in government and business and cultural life. We weren't engaged in advocacy journalism. We were reporting what the laws allowed, how bureaucracies were denying certain costly benefits to keep their budgets in balance – instead of finding ways to comply with the law. (Mencken thought do-gooders – including do-good reporters -- needed to get over themselves.) We thought we were reminding readers and editors of a newspaper's role: "light for all" as the *Sun* of Baltimore put it. Wasn't that our job?

With a half-century of journalism behind me, I have to thank the UNC journalism professor in the modified clown suit, who hooked me with the assignments he gave.

I found I could see and hear and think productively about events I was sent to cover. I could see stories in the chaos. There is a step between an assignment and translating what you found on the street into a story that someone might want to read. There was a cerebral chemistry there. I hadn't known. I wasn't aware of the story process, the seeing and translating the elements into narrative. I didn't know that I was mixing and matching and flipping and thinking about how to begin. Not with once upon a time, but something like a crystallization that led to the "lede," the first paragraph, the hook, the words that said, "This way to the candy store." I was "always working" even before I was working.

Tribune

Gene Farrell hadn't pressed to know why I wanted to be a reporter and maybe that was a good thing. I would have told him: I thought I could be every reader's, every citizen's representative. I could report while they worked. I wanted that responsibility the way the All Saints Day woman cherished her one-day-a-year responsibility. I'm not sure where this aspect of the calling came from. Could have been a civics course with significant treatment of how the democracy depends on a vigorous press. As I thought about it, I began to see myself in the role of tribune. My very modest inner self again.

The responsibility was there by definition. I had the role like it or not. The realization made the learning curve less steep. I could write a little, but I would have to be much better, faster and more discerning. I could never be satisfied, an easy goal to reach – but I only got there a few times. Getting to the point of meeting my goal – along with the thrill of occasionally writing a good lede – I would succeed, as a friend of mine put it much later, because the newspaper /democracy gods were watching over me.

Over the years, people needled me about being a member of the Fourth Estate. The tone would be jocular but approving. I see it now as a kind of buy-in, an acceptance by them and by me. I tried not to betray my ready embrace of that role.

Of course, I didn't march out every day with the First Amendment ringing in my ears. I was pulled along by the daily demands and by the prospect of another bit of amazing news, another wreath full of dollars for the priest, another pious believer on a holy mission.

Overtime

I clipped every one of the first stories I wrote. I pasted them in a dark green scrap book. Some were no more than three or four inches long. It seems a little embarrassing looking back, but other journalists were similarly besotted with their earliest production.

H. L. Mencken, for example. After his first stories, he wrote:

> I was up with the milkman the next morning to search the paper, and when I found both of my pieces, exactly as written, there ran such thrills through my system as a barrel of brandy and 100,000 volts of electricity could not have matched.

Mencken recounts as well the work that went into these first two printed paragraphs: "...I wrote and tore up, wrote and tore up," he says in his *Newspaper Days*. Really? His copy did not spring full-blown from his soon-to-be-revered forehead? Good to know.

I had seen the Mencken technique exercised by mere newspaper mortals. I came to work one day to find balled up pages of a sports story that began, "It wasn't the best of times..." and then "It was neither the best nor the worst of times for the Jersey City Ducks as they fought valiantly against their Newark rivals." One could use the universally known phrases of literature without fear of committing plagiarism. Readers would know what you were doing. They would see nothing more than a tribute to the great Dickens whose prose could be borrowed occasionally to give a baseball game and a newspaper hack a way into another game story and maybe a bit of class.

Writing and tearing up or leaning on one of the greats was the name of the game. You were looking for your own style. Somewhere you heard that meshing your style with the newspaper's style, or UPI's style but there was no enforcing of such a requirement if such a requirement ever existed.

On occasion as I wrote and tore up, I stayed late. I would have stayed late every day except for the question:

"You on overtime?"

"No," I said. I think I was expecting to be praised for my industriousness. Instead I was, once again, about to learn something important about newspapers, their history, newspapermen – and life itself.

"So, you're working for nothing," said this old hand whose name I have forgotten if I ever knew it. Yes, I think I might have said, once again showing my great dedication to the craft. But it wasn't a question. It was a statement with a purpose I did not immediately see.

I was perfecting something I had written, working hard, and offering what bosses demanded. What I demanded. It was adrenaline to me. I wanted to please myself, to have the sentences flow and sparkle if sparkle was appropriate. I wanted to push back and read the paragraph over and over. I thought I knew the path. I had to work hard. I had to stay late. The good old Protestant work ethic was no friend of the family. Missing dinner with their families? Reporters had done that forever – or lost their jobs when they refused. (I started to understand the upbraiding I was getting after I got married. Would I be home for dinner? How could we really live on $75-a-week plus my new wife's substitute teacher pay?) Now, after years of bruising conflict, there was a union that could protect us if we were willing to protect and police ourselves.

So, clueless newbies like me were not going to undermine the new rules.

The scruffy guy with the mustache, the re-write master and some of the editors, only recently having moved up from reporting or copy-editing ranks, would not allow it.

They had new power. They would shut the place down if management didn't see the justice in their demands. They had risked their jobs by merely thinking that a union was necessary. They were not happy with newcomers, single and hard-charging, who were willing to do for nothing what they had struggled to avoid: work without pay. A new friend and veteran of the union-building days urged me to always get paid for some story or other – a story I would have been overjoyed simply to see in print. Your writing is your livelihood, he said. It's your life, your future. Take what you've earned. So, they shooed me out of the newsroom. Over time, I would see even more clearly what our forebears had done for us.

12

Eddie

Still, there were times when I found myself in the office late. And on one of these nights I learned how the paper came out.

Eddie brought it out. Short and lean, he had a certain sharp-eyed countenance discernible through the distortions of drink. He was a prodigious consumer, arriving on his own around midnight or accepting the help of a copy boy sent to fetch him from a saloon, his hangout, near the paper.

He rolled into the newsroom with a too-happy smile on his face. He looked around for someone to greet. He was looking for a kind of approval: If someone would listen to him maybe he wasn't too drunk to actually be there. One of the new men would be just the ticket. The new men! One night it was me. I wasn't likely to be asking him any questions. Pipe firmly clenched in his teeth, he began to declaim about something.

"The gllibthi hardy every worse, know?"

I nodded.

"And nobus anywys. I'm right?"

I nodded. He went on for some time before smiling and moving off toward the library.

Tom O'Keefe, the re-write man, walked quietly over to me.

"Don't tell anyone what Eddie said," he whispered.

There was a slight grin on his face. He knew I hadn't understood a single word. O'Keefe walked back to his typewriter, stifling a giggle.

Eddie, I noticed, headed toward the library where the clips and photographs were stored. Stories were wrapped around the one-column "cut" – the metal upon which a photograph had been embossed. Clip and cut, paper and metal, were secured with a rubber band and tucked into a small heavy paper jacket. Pretty sophisticated and technological.

Old stories were not Eddie's goal. He was headed for the Hilton Room. I never heard it called the morgue, though it probably had that tag earlier. The *Jersey Journal's* version was named (informally) for the tiny woman, in her 70s, who kept it as pristine as a hospital's operating theater.

I followed Eddie at a distance. There were desks adjacent to the stacks of clipping files but they had nothing on them. Perhaps Ms. Hilton, Molly by name, knew how these tables were to be used when she wasn't there.

Eddie's condition might have been concerning. Quite the contrary. Everything was going as it always did. Only if he didn't show at all would anyone begin to fret.

There were two or three long, potential beds, free of everything. The "rag files" – a week or two of the most recent papers kept for quick reference during the day – were off to the side. The tables were just about long enough to accommodate a man of Eddie's height. I watched him stretch out on one of them, fold his hands over his chest and close his eyes.

He slept for an hour, until 1 a.m. or so and then, without benefit of alarm clock, arose, walked to his chair in the newsroom and put out the paper. He had heroic, even legendary recuperative powers.

The silly smile was gone now and if he was in hangover pain it was not visible. He had been paying the price of over-imbibing for years. He was saved also by the routine. He looked at the wires. He looked at the local file. He chose a lead story. He had no second thoughts. He was the man. He had followed this course for years.

Everyone knew Eddie came to work drunk, and sleeping some of it off in the library, and coming to the managing editor's post hung over, was routine. Eddie was Eddie, part of the system, indispensable and widely praised for his cool command. Amusing to me now that I should have met Eddie in the first paper I worked for. In the years that followed I only met one or two other reporters (or editors) who fit the drinking part of our collective popular identity. (In two of the papers, alcoholism could lead to company-financed treatment. Jobs were held pending the patient's return. This part of the system went back to the time when the newspaperman stereotype was more accurate.)

Eddie might not have made it, actually, as the years went by save for Augustin Torres, a copy kid then who would walk across the street, find Eddie and escort him to the newsroom. Torres' ease and availability for whatever he might be asked to do helped no doubt as he moved up from copy kid to chief political writer. Upward, stumbling, steadying mobility was also part of the system.

13

Dog and Pony Show

In 1965, Gene Farrell and Thomas Gangemi, mayor of Jersey City, conspired to produce a calamitous dog and pony show: a contrivance, offered as news but a thinly veiled way of making the author look good or dynamic or creative.

In this case, mayor and editor would fly or sail to Genoa, Italy, to fetch one Cristoforo Colombo and bring him to America to serve as grand marshal of the 1965 Columbus Day Parade.

Colombo's appeal seemed to be simply his name or maybe he was a descendant. We didn't get that far into the story.

All of this proceeded without a murmur of concern from anyone on the paper as far as I could tell. I was green but I knew mayors and editors didn't go star shopping whatever the holiday. Suddenly, a newspaper was setting aside its independence to join the mayor in a grand public relations stunt.

A conflict of interest on its face, a slippery slope, a bad idea for the mayor as well – as events would show.

Fun and games, you say. No harm, no foul. But didn't it open the newspaper to criticism and consternation?

For Farrell, the Columbus Day caper fit a pattern. He had decided how Jersey City would honor JFK. He had started something called "Women of Achievement," recognition for women then still minimized in a community's business life; a Spelling Bee, a Science Fair and a Father and Sons Sports Banquet.

He served at various points in his life on at least two important governing bodies: the N.J. Public Market Commission and the Jersey City Medical Center's Board of Managers. How could he be expected to write critically about a public body he served on?

Newsroom veterans remembered Farrell as someone willing to accept or even solicit the odd freebie: movie tickets and the like. Just little things, right?

"You can't buy me with a dinner or a movie ticket," a recipient was likely to say.

Those questions, unasked, left an aura of small-bore corruption in the minds of *Journal* reporters. Some of the Farrell stories truly were harmless, the kind of anecdotal history everyone revels in.

The "milk run," for example.

What *Journal* reporters remembered most vividly was the "milk run." A reporter drove to Farrell's house sometime after midnight to pick up his editorials for the next day's paper. You didn't go to the front door. You stumbled around in the dark to the milk box in the back. You felt around for the pages and took them back to the paper. But not right away.

Torres made a routine of it. When he was a copyboy, he delivered the edits to Journal Square after grabbing two dozen donuts, one dozen for the guys at the *Hudson Dispatch*, a *Journal* competitor, and one for the lobster shift guys at the *Journal*. Torres and the others who made the run picked up an early edition of the *Dispatch* to see if it had a story the *Journal* had missed. Theoretically, this meant the *Journal* could never get "beat" – missing a story run by the *Dispatch,* one of its competitors in the halcyon days of papers. Back at the *Journal*, someone would make sure the missing story, if any, was matched in time for the *Journal's* first edition.

Torres recited the Farrell folklore: Gene and Lois enjoyed movies but didn't like to pay. A news reporter would be assigned by Fegan to call the movie house in question, report the imminent arrival of the *Journal's* editor and ask if tickets could be ready for them.

Harvey Zucker, who arrived at the paper as Farrell was retiring, said Farrell had certain ideas about what made a story and what didn't. Zucker had been sent out to write about the mass exodus of store owners from a building on Journal Square. A book store, a dentist and several other old establishments were leaving. Their rents had suddenly been doubled.

Farrell, sitting in for a vacationing assignment editor, killed the story: Rents go up all the time, he said. He told Zucker he had called the property owners. They were not charging unreasonable rents.

They were simply bringing them up to market rate. But even if he was right, wasn't it still a story – with the departure of so many well-known long-term establishments people relied on? Did the story need more reporting? Whatever, spiking it was not the answer.

When the vacationing editor returned, the story ran.

As for the Colombo show, everything seemed to be falling into place.

The elegant Gangemi, slender and handsome, would stride along in the parade doffing his snappy straw boater, flanked by Mr. Colombo and Farrell. A (papal) purple stripe had been painted down the center of the parade route.

The paper covered Gangemi as mayor, of course. Nat Berg, the paper's political writer and a caricature of a caricature, had written about him repeatedly. Berg spoke out of the side of his mouth, eyes darting left and right as if someone might be walking up behind him. He never looked at you. Years earlier, he had been Mr. Fixit. (I hadn't known this at the time. Had I been on some sort of critical path leading to political reporter?)

Sometimes such profiles ran under the headline:

"He's the News."

They didn't pretend to show much more than a new title or promotion someone had earned. They tended to be *pro forma* and short. The seriousness of profile writing grew immensely more important over my time in the business. Days and weeks were spent finding out everything about the profile subject. The newspaper's job was to report carefully and fully on anyone who wanted to manage the people's money and play an official role in a city or state's future.

A thorough Gangemi piece would have been illuminating. He had started a fruit and vegetable business at the age of 16. He did well and subsequently ran for mayor several times. He had previously won elective posts in the county government. Then, in 1961, he was elected mayor of Jersey City.

But there was more to know.

14

Little Big Man

Gangemi's winning was thought to be the work of John V. Kenny, the Hudson County political boss, who succeeded Boss Hague. No one got elected to anything without the diminutive Kenny.

"If you've got 'The Little Guy'," it was said in the political world, "you don't need anyone else. If you don't have him, the good Lord be with you."

When he was mayor, "Kenny could be found each day on Pavonia Avenue at the corner of Erie. He used to stand on the walk in the mornings and in the day with his constituents," said a New Jersey native who got his dockworker's union book, not from a union guy, but from Kenny. The pol sold them on the street for a discounted price of $250, big money then.

From his perch just to the waterfront side of St. Michael's Church, the parish's leading benefactor (Kenny) dispensed jobs and good counsel while collecting what he was owed under the kickback system Hague had perfected. JVK had become nothing short of a racketeer. Every aspect of government seems to have been seen for decades in Jersey City as an opportunity for graft.

Hague had named Kenny leader of the city's Second Ward in 1931, making him first among equals in the machine's upper echelon. "The Little Guy" became the unofficial boss of Local 1247, a longshoremen's local. He had cornered the market. He became a *de facto* union boss. He had been a bookkeeper for the nearby Erie Railroad. Kenny's father left him money earned as the proprietor of several saloons. His already ample portion would grow.

Jersey City employees were expected to kick back a percentage of their wages. They did this each month on "rice pudding day," a term meaning something like (financial) dessert. The name carried a certain haughty laugh at the idea of honest government. Kenny probably earned far more from their control of something called the "loading racket." It was a system that guaranteed them a piece of every exchange made between rail car, truck and barge.

Kenny allowed jobs to be lost to his city when he insisted on keeping control of hiring and firing at the port. The government promised to leave with its jobs if he didn't relent. He did not. The jobs moved to another state. "Rule or ruin" was not a familiar term for me then. Kenny employed it whatever the cost.

The who, what, where orders did not always allow larger truths to emerge.

This empire was Kenny's as Democratic Party leader in Hudson County while Gangemi was mayor. On that night in Gangemi's court, Kenny interrupted quietly. An unnamed observer told the story to Anthony Olszewski, a county historian writing in 2004 for the Hudson County Politics Message board. I know of no other account. He does not identify his source. But the citizenship issue proved all too true.

"Mayor", Kenny said, "there's a couple of papers here I'd like you to take a look at."

Gangemi turned on him.

"Hey, you, I'm the mayor now. You sit down. I'll see you when I'm good and ready."

Kenny sat. He said something to himself, something overheard by one of the bystanders.

"That's right. You're the mayor now." He put his hat on his knee and waited.

By the time he finished, Gangemi seemed a bit nervous. In a friendly voice, he asked Kenny what he wanted. Kenny stood up. He handed the mayor a file folder.

After glancing at the papers, Gangemi said OK and began to apologize. For what, no one knew. The next day the confrontation was all the talk. If anyone thought the "little guy" was losing his edge, this moment said otherwise.

Gangemi had gotten a letter from the U.S. State Department. A shortened version of its contents: "You cannot get a passport because you are not a citizen of the United States." Actually, he was born in Calabria, Italy. He arrived in the U.S. at age 10.

What candidate for mayor or other high office could get so far with no one knowing he was not a citizen – not knowing, that is, where the candidate was born?

The importance of the word "now" in Kenny's "You're the mayor now" became clearer. Questions about Gangemi's citizenship had arisen before in Jersey City politics. True or not, it hadn't mattered. Kenny won or his anointed men won.

Kenny must have known. Like bosses who demanded resignation letters as insurance against disobedience, he sat on the information 'til he needed it.

Kenny "dropped the dime" on Gangemi. (The term referred to the cost when the term was invented of a phone call to the authorities.) Kenny called Washington, where his power in New Jersey gave him all the entre he needed.

When the story broke, Kenny acted as if he was shocked, even sympathetic. He had, after all, endorsed the man.

"I'm sure Mayor Gangemi thought he was a citizen," Kenny told the newspapers. "It must be a terrible shock to him to discover the State Department questions his status." You could almost hear "the Little Guy" laughing.

This wasn't the first time Kenny had been able to get the help he needed. When Adlai Stevenson was running for president in the 1950s, Kenny wanted the Democratic contender to pay his respects – to meet Kenny at Kenny's home. The shiny bright Stevenson said no, no doubt having heard of Kenney's reputation. But Kenny managed to hijack the candidate's motorcade and guide it to the appointed front porch where Kenny waved smilingly. The Boss got the photograph he wanted. Stevenson went on his way. Other candidates were more willing to pose with the county leader – better that than lose the voting support the Kenny machine could deliver.

The soon-to-be unfrocked mayor summoned members of the city council to his room at Harkness Pavilion, Presbyterian Medical Center in Manhattan to explain what was happening. He was said to be suffering from the effects of immunizations given in anticipation of the trip to Italy. More likely, he was suffering from humiliation and taking refuge where he might find some sympathy. He resigned officially on September 26, 1963.

The story was covered, mostly, by Richard Sapir, a frenetic and temperamental young reporter who sat in the middle of the newsroom, twirling the hair on the top of his head with one hand while he wrote. Once a week or so, Sapir – affronted by some unknown slight – would phone in from a bar to resign. Apparently determined to have the newspaper demonstrate its love for his talents, the threat seemed enough to keep him going. As it turns out, Jersey City survived without a mayor for 47 days as various forces maneuvered to get their chosen successor into the office. The council, which had to choose a successor, could not agree.

Finally, one of their own, Councilman Tom Whelan, emerged as the council's choice. History alone suggested there was trouble ahead for him. the *Wall Street Journal* wondered in a headline if the new mayor could "escape the alluring past." Almost no one had in that era or those to follow.

Farrell's dog and pony Columbus Day show brought the sharpest focus on city government and politics. As newspapers became more aggressive, stories like the mayor's lack of citizenship were broken not by the bosses but by reporters thirsting for what one of my colleagues likes to call "roof" – stories that raised the roof.

15

Thomas Aquinas

I thought I remembered meeting Whelan at his home. He lived in a part of Jersey City I had never seen. It was not far from the newspaper offices on Journal Square, which was part of the district he represented in the council. I knew he had been a pilot in WWII, that he was a vice president at the phone company. He had a perfect political resume – war hero, former high school athlete, family man. He had run for political office only once and now there was some noise that he might be the one to break the council impasse – that he might be the city's next mayor. He had not been connected publicly with Kenny.

But he was one of the only council members who chose not to visit Gangemi on the occasion of the mayor's forced abdication. Had someone whispered in his ear? Don't look sympathetic to Kenny's enemy.

I was sent to interview him.

He was a physically impressive guy. Well over 6 feet tall, as outgoing as a phone company exec – or a politician – should be. He got quickly to the point he wanted to make: he was a spiritual man, a thinking man, a man who read to deepen his faith. Several times, he came back to his penchant for contemplation and a thoughtful consideration of life. St. Thomas Aquinas was the writer who spoke to him, he said.

He knew he was being assessed by the newspaper and by the voters who hardly knew him. There was no immediate reason to think of him as a protégé of Kenny's and thus a threat to the public treasury. Writers at other papers suggested that any new mayor, whatever his reading taste, would have trouble staying honest in Jersey City.

My story appeared several days later with a photo of Whelan and his family – wife and children. Near the end of the story was a line accentuating his determination to introduce himself as a man who, I wrote, "loved to think."

Instead, my story said "loved to "thump." This verb followed the names and ages of his many children.

16

The Metallic Mantis

Somewhere in the editing process or in the production process, in the dimly lit factory-like rooms off to the right of the newsroom, someone had had a bit of fun. At Whelan's expense and maybe at mine as well.

Would I be held responsible for naughty or suggestive language? Would I be able to find the "copy" – the ink-on-paper story with all of its editing? (In the digital world of course, there would be no question. The entire life of that story, version by version from my desk to the copy desk to the composing/production rooms would be instantly available. The perpetrator could be quickly located. Not so then.)

I walked up the stairs that morning with some trepidation. Surely, there would be some accounting.

But no one seemed to have noticed. No one mentioned it to me, at any rate. People had other, more pressing stuff to do. I'd be hearing from someone. I thought I should find out what happened. Where had "thump" come from?

I walked into the room with the linotype machines, a cacophony of jarring sound welling toward me. (In Baltimore, I learned later, many of the linotype operators were deaf.)

I began to think that the men who put the newspaper together were not without their ways and means, their freedom to add a bit of an editorial comment, a kind of wry observation. I imagined someone thinking to himself:

"Yeah, Whelan, big deal thinker. My ass is a big thinker. We know you and your father and your brother. Not a thinker in the bunch far as I'm concerned."

I walked hesitantly through the room, past the many machines and realizing I couldn't make an issue of an egregious junior high school-like shenanigan. If that's what it was. Not only that, I learned later I was trespassing. These were carefully guarded union precincts. Interlopers were regarded with suspicion – in part because the work was so exacting it could tolerate no outsiders.

No one needed some new reporter asking outrageous questions. Still.

I was instantly in awe of these machines, totally distracted. They had elaborate if spindly shoulders and gripping feet that kept the complex enterprise anchored. I have thought of them ever since as akin to a giant, metallic praying mantis.

They had not one but two keyboards and a single arm or wing. The machine operated in a sliding, stopping and starting sequence that seemed to have, notwithstanding its girth and odor of hot lead, a symphonic elegance. The cooperator kept it all moving. Below the single wing, amid a layered set of shuttles and shifters, lay a small furnace capable of up to 500 degrees heat, sufficient to produce lines embossed with letters.

The linotype operators I had glimpsed were men of singular concentration, often wearing green eyeshades. They were the link between reporters and editors and the production system seen by virtually no one. They typed slowly, accurately and patiently, producing the lines of lead, each one carrying a word, or parts of a word, each line a sentence, each stack of lines a paragraph.

The operators had to be wordsmiths of another kind. They had to know how words divide so that the breaks were in the right place, falling over one line onto the next. If they made mistakes and there was time before deadline, the line of type would have to be re-set. Ideally. There was great pride here, even if the occasional mischief was exerted. The right decisions had to be made quickly.

At the *Baltimore Sun,* I would learn many years later, management had been deeply suspicious of the new machines. Despite the new speed, the paper's owners were conservative. They adopted the devices but slowly. Years later copy editors said to me when I wanted to alter some nuance of style. "Type is not made of rubber." That moment of instruction should have been another lesson, but mostly it came to me as part of a brew of brain cells and brawn that, somehow, landed on the street in seven different editions every day.

Some years later, the *Washington Post* shined up an old machine and placed it in the paper's lobby, giving honor to its revolutionary importance to the business and to its inventor Otto Mergenthaler. Thomas Edison called him a genius.

Now and then, the think and thump and linotype episode comes back to me. When I began checking some of my memories, I eagerly anticipated finding the story in the Jersey City library's voluminous archive of political corruption coverage.

Not there. Not in the file, not in the microfilm – unless I missed it. None of the stories I did find mentioned Whelan's devotion to Thomas Aquinas. Had I dreamed or confabulated the whole thing? I had done a story about a large family but there was no think or thump or Aquinas. We all know of course that memory is faulty and even crafty.

I was absolutely right about one thing: In Jersey City, corruption came with the territory. A few years after his election, Whelan and Kenny went to jail. That apparently predictable result gave Whelan more time with his mentor Aquinas.

17

A Ridiculous Number

With Whelan heading for his reward, I was sent to the newspaper's Bayonne Bureau. The suburb-like town was known mostly for its famous steel-arch bridge to Staten Island. Its natives included Barney Frank, the congressman later from Massachusetts and Frank Langella, the actor. The newspaper publisher S.I. Newhouse, who owned a chain of newspapers, including the *Jersey Journal,* had lived there. His empire later included the *New Yorker.*

The journal's bureau occupied a gun barrel storefront office, handily just across from city hall and the courthouse.

The bureau chief, Al Ciaburri, came by every evening around 6 after he bought the *New York Daily News.* We wouldn't see him before then. He'd amble up to the door in his raincoat, step just inside the door and, holding the paper by a corner and out away from his body, he'd ask: "Is that the most ridiculous number you ever heard of?"

A "reasonable" number would have been the one in the newspaper if it matched the number Al had in his pocket, the one that recorded his little bet.

"The Number" was the pari-mutuel number reported every afternoon on the sports page. "The Number" aka "The Handle" was the total amount of money wagered that day at one of the local tracks. Ciaburri always had a little money in the illegal game. This of course was before every state in the nation got into the numbers business, a business states had always regarded as a criminal activity.

He didn't buy the paper for the news. He didn't even want to see what the competition was doing in the other local paper. It was all about The Number and his little act in the doorway.

If he had won, if the number had not been "ridiculous," his life would have changed. I wondered if having the money would have been as satisfying to him as making the daily visit to his bureau, performing his little soft shoe in the doorway, thinking of himself as the perpetual underdog. He would have missed that celebration of life as he knew it.

"What's going on?" Al asked after we'd seen he hadn't won yet again.

I'd been in the court that afternoon. I was there to see what would happen to an older kid who'd driven his car down Bayonne Boulevard at 60 or 70 miles an hour, crashed several blocks north of the bureau office. I'd heard the car roar by and then heard the crash as I ran up there expecting to see a lot of injured people. A few were loaded into a city ambulance.

And now the driver's day in court.

"Reckless little shit," cops in the back of the room said.

"Way above the speed limit, your honor," another cop said.

The kid didn't have a lawyer. The judge asked if he had anything to say.

"Fuck you," the kid said.

The cop in the witness stand started to come down and slap the kid.

A bailiff stepped in the way.

The kid, protected now, addressing the cop, "You're so brave, riding around in your gum ball machine." (A gumball machine was a police car with flashing light on top.) The kid's friends smirked in admiration behind him.

"What'd they do with him?" Ciaburri asked.

"Thirty days in juvie," I said.

"What else is going on?" he asked.

I told him about a love nest kids had made out of cardboard.

"A love den?" he said. "A cardboard condo?" Ciaburri said.

"Yes, kids go there to make out," I said.

"I want it," he said. "With art." (Photographs)

"Anybody thinking about an editorial?" he wondered.

"Maybe," I said.

"Nothing controversial," Al said. Maybe something about a reading program at the library, something about a campaign to end illiteracy, maybe. Something like that.

"Or write your story about the condo and then write an editorial about that," he said.

So, I'd been doing nothing but obituaries and there I was, after Kennedy's death and the Gangemi thing, writing about love dens. Somebody had to cover Bayonne. No one was going to give me Jersey City politics. But I was seeing why bigger newspapers wanted reporters to work a few years in places like Bayonne. You got a chance to do everything – editorials, cops, the courts, literacy programs.

(I hadn't known Ciaburri at all before being sent out to the bureau. Many years later, researching this memoir, I discovered he had something I had wanted: a byline on the Kennedy assassination story. Al and another reporter had their names on the "react" piece we'd all been sent out to do. He had been here long enough to get the prize, your name above the story, this one about a slain president.)

18

The Bard

In Jersey City, beginning in 1960, the newspaper sponsored a spelling bee. It was another of the extracurriculars designed to generate drama, to involve young readers and to serve as a contribution to the community. Then of course someone had to write about it – constantly. There were stories about the contest rules. Stories about past winners and what the bee had meant to them in their lives. There were profiles of the organizers. Profiles of the contestants, dramatic re-plays of the final moments of an earlier year's contest, photos of the winners, reports of their trips to Washington and pictures of them and their families touring the White House, one of the prizes. We all had a turn looking for angles.

Ozzie Johnston's idea was inspired. He had come to the newspaper from Harvard University after some years of struggling to finish (or start) a Ph.D. in 18th and 19th century English literature. Byron was his subject. It wasn't happening. He was achieving the ABD status – All But Dissertation. The whole subject had, finally, begun to weigh on him. "How could this have happened to me?" He had always known some form of brain freeze or burnout was a possibility. But maybe it was more than that, more than some high level of writers' cramp. Maybe he had begun to realize the world of Byron scholarship wasn't exactly what he wanted.

So, he decided to try newspapers. He arrived in Jersey City with the usual fanfare – which was no fanfare at all. He was not your run-of-the-mill newshound in waiting. He had that slightly burned-out look of the library mole. His hair was lank and long, maybe in need of a wash, spilling over his forehead, threatening to obscure his vision. And yet there he was, reborn as it were, with confidence gained from his breakout decision.

"How'd you end up here?" Farrell asked. Surely, he had contacts around Harvard Square. Well, yes, but they weren't newspaper contacts, Ozzie said. Probably not, Farrell probably said to himself.

"I need to get some experience," he said, leveling with Farrell. Ozzie gave us the rest of the sentence. He was putting himself on the fast track. He didn't have a lot of time for interning or apprenticing.

"I'm going to get a little experience before I become too expensive," he said. He thought some good newspaper would hire him when he couldn't command much of a salary. With experience, his graduate degrees might push him toward a higher, unaffordable, salary. So, Farrell was getting a Harvard guy on the cheap. Like me, a Carolina gentleman, he was a more than willing participant in the polite scramble for assignments, the ones that seemed to be sensible and necessary and those that seemed lame.

The *Jersey Journal* spelling bee, for example. For this, Ozzie set out to demonstrate a truism of reporting: better to have an idea of your own than wait for some editor to offer his or hers. Yours were always better. You got a little more freedom. Editors began to rely on you. Ozzie seemed to know this instinctively, a little earlier than the rest of us.

Thus did he suggest an interview with a certified descendant of William Shakespeare who, Ozzie said he had learned, was due to arrive from London at the Newark airport. The *Jersey Journal* would be getting a manufactured exclusive. Of course, it was. There was no Shakespeare relative, no flight from London, no known survivor of the Bard. There was just Ozzie and his determination to breathe life into a spelling bee.

Why Jersey City?

What fun. Didn't the Bard's descendant have his pick of cities with spelling bees? Why had he chosen Jersey City of all places? What hidden attribute accounted for this fancy? Ozzie set out to hear whatever the great man's relative had to say about Jersey City – and, of course, anything else Ozzie would have him declaiming about.

Yes, you could make stuff up. Lesser scribes than the Bard of Baltimore had done it. Newspapers were moving decidedly away from that sort of thing

– and yet you could still do it if it was pretty clear that everyone, including primarily the readers, would know you were doing it.

Within a few weeks, it turned out, Ozzie was off to the *Baltimore Sun*.

I suppose, looking back, I might have had some competitive pangs. Why wasn't I moving? Well, Ozzie was older and wearing some academic cred well beyond my own.

And there was another thing. I had just gotten married. Martha Hayes was an airline stewardess living in Manhattan. We met at a party, started seeing each other and, after an on and off romance, decided to marry. We found an apartment not far from the newspaper on John F. Kennedy Boulevard. She was all-in for me and newspapers. She began substitute teaching in Rahway, several stops south on the New Jersey Turnpike.

We had friends in Syosset, New York. Martha's stewardess friend Pat's husband owned a clothing store and lived in a grand house with a swimming pool. I remember being there one afternoon when the Israelis were winning the Six-Day War in 1967. Pat's husband was Jewish so the atmosphere was decidedly celebratory. We went out to dinner. They all had drinks and steak. We drank water with our pasta. When the bill came, we split it so the guardian-of-democracy reporter helped pay for the clothing magnate's dinner: My reporter's $70-a-week budget exploded. I had to borrow money for the George Washington Bridge toll.

I cared then and later about the quality of the newspaper that I did about income disparities.

Like everything else, the quality of newspapers varied. The ones I worked for later would never have operated the way the *Journal* under Farrell did. But the *Jersey Journal* was still an important, indispensable monitor of civic life. Papers that played less carefully with their franchise were still important players. "The Joisey," for example, had endorsed Frank Hague in 1917 when he first ran but backed off later when it saw a mayor who spent more time in Florida or New York City than in the city he'd been elected to lead.

John Lancelotti, a little older and more experienced than I, offered me a version of the newsman's quotidian ethic one day: "You had to work as hard on the one or two or three-graf story as you did on the longer, more substantive ones. Get something wrong on a story that seemed inconsequential and you were gambling with the readers' trust. The little stories were sometimes the ones people knew something about. Maybe you understood the big picture pretty well, but if you blew it on the little things people would notice."

No one had appointed Lancelotti czar of newsroom values. No one said, "You, Lancelotti, make sure the new boys understand how we operate." No one would have risked acting like the sergeant at arms in charge of the newspaperman's conscience. He did it anyway, as did others when they thought it necessary.

Newspaper people, Lancelotti went on, were some of the "cleanest" – he meant honest – people you were going to meet in life. Really? How could he know, I wondered at the time? What other groups did he have for comparative purposes? As my experience grew, I began to see he was right. I also knew people on the outside would have guffawed. We never wrote about ourselves, so how could they know?

The stereotypes – etched more deeply in the public mind by isolated cases of unprincipled and dishonest practice – may have been embraced even more firmly in recent times. Yet, we hardly ever defended ourselves against any criticism – that we were gossip mongers with no values. We didn't want to be special pleaders in an over-hyped world. We thought we could adequately represent ourselves every day in everything we did. The paper was our defense. Our work would speak for itself. People would see.

We had the image of special pleaders despite our rejecting of that idea. We came across as proud of our untouchability. I plead guilty. I was proud of my humility. Oddly, I thought, since we were news gatherers, we were more than a little isolated. We didn't see what was happening to us – not until our existence was threatened.

We made the mistake political candidates make when they don't respond to damaging criticism: Never let the opponent define you.

True to my old news guy's instruction, I started looking for another job two years after I landed in Journal Square. (I had my concerns about Farrell, but

I knew I wasn't staying with this paper.) I started looking, sending out letters to papers all over, principally the *Denver Post* and the *Providence Journal*. These were papers where I could get more seasoning, more responsibility. The *Post* sent me what amounted to an open book, take-home public affairs test. I don't know how editors there could learn much from such an exercise because, of course, you could look up the answers. Maybe there was a time limit. Maybe you were honor bound not to cheat. Anyway, a *Post* editor told me I had scored about as well on the test as anyone he could remember. I thanked Mr. Fixit. Most of the questions were assessing general knowledge I had dealt with while responding to inquiries for kids writing term papers in Jersey City.

At about this time, I heard from the paper in Providence.

"Yes, we have an opening. Can you come up here for an interview?"

Of course, I could. The next day. Right there and then, the Providence paper offered me a job. I may have thought about it for a minute. Denver had its allure, the Rockies and all. But Providence was an easier move and I'd heard it was a good paper. Marty Gately, another of the editors who looked at you, if at all, over his bi-focals, said Providence had been well thought-of. Then he said something about how difficult it was getting through the city of Providence on the way to Boston. (I-95 was then nearing completion).

That was pretty much my "goodbye." I don't remember any conversation with Farrell. My bad. I owed him a lot. He gave me a chance.

When I went back to "da Joisey" in 2015, I was unable to find his obituary – in his newspaper. Microfilm copies of the paper were in the city library, not the newsroom. Clips as well. I couldn't find a Farrell obit. There must have been one. (I later found one online.) Probably made a pretty good feature – if anyone had a picture.

Part II:

The *Providence Journal*

1965-1977

19

The Boy Next Door

The *Journal* sent me to its bureau in Attleboro, just over the Rhode Island/Massachusetts line. I covered everything: school board, zoning board, board of selectmen (city council), features, obituaries – and Vietnam War's home front.

One of my first stories was a feature obituary: Joe Nimiroski was the first soldier from Attleboro to die in Vietnam. He was killed just before Christmas, 1965.

A Marine honor guard delivered the news at 2 a.m., December 19, a day after his death.

Alice Nimiroski woke to a knocking at her door. She came downstairs in her bathrobe.

Two young men in full military dress came into her living room, hats under their arms. They stood at attention in front of a shimmering artificial silver Christmas tree.

Of course, she knew why they were there before they spoke. Or maybe Joe was just wounded? But no. Corporal Joseph Elwin Nimiroski had been killed in a four hour battle at Ky Phu, Quang Nam Province, December 18, 1965 The Marines didn't want Mrs. Nimiroski to learn of her son's death on the TV news or in the morning newspaper.

Her son had been a first. And she would be one of the first parents to host a bereavement team. Soon, mothers and fathers with a son or daughter in uniform, would be haunted by the prospect of such a visit. These private, devastating ceremonies were joined in the public mind by a succession of momentum-building anti-war images: body bags arriving at Dover Air Force

Base in Delaware, a mass rally in Central Park, a March on the Pentagon, takeovers of college presidents' offices.

Alice's other son, Tim, came into the room as the Marines spoke. He stood next to his mother. No one in the Nimiroski family questioned the visit's 2 a.m. timing. Or why Joe's mother and not his new wife, Valerie, was the first to know of his death. In the fog of war all information may not be disseminated quickly. A telegram came later – a second jolt of the new reality – as if the family might think the earlier visit was a mistake.

Alice and Tim remembered what Joe had told them a few months earlier. He found the war incomprehensible: not enough fire power, not enough effort to win. Why have a war if we didn't try to win? And then, they must have thought, after all the questions, becoming a victim. What must he have been thinking in the midst of battle. Another 57,000 Americans would die in spite of more and more artillery, more and more troops – never enough.

I remember wondering as they spoke: What could a 22-year-old know about leadership's thinking, a commander's tactics, geopolitical considerations?

I listened to their story with more personal experience than many reporters would have had. I'd been to Vietnam – briefly.

Two years before Joe's arrival there, with a contingent of sergeants and higher ranking officers, I flew to bases all over Southeast Asia: South Korea, Thailand, the Philippines and Vietnam.

Did these bases have the mega compressors and other equipment needed to get our planes started and in the air?

"It's all there on the books," I said to one of the sergeants.

"You have to see it," he said.

We made our way from the contingency bases to the chaotic gearing-up. We saw the incongruously European-looking tropical city, Saigon. We had dinner at a nice French restaurant. We scanned the wide boulevards. We were a step up from tourists. We heard stories about the guerilla hand grenade attacks just starting on buses in the city. We left the war having no idea of its rending future.

What could a 22-year-old kid know about a war even as he faced it? More than most, I learned from his mother.

"His teachers at the Thatcher School were amazed at how much he knew about wars," she told me. He had a library of books on World Wars I and II and Korea.

"He wanted to be a member of an elite corps," his brother said. "If you didn't understand, he would spend an hour or two explaining."

In the first year of his Vietnam tour, his father died. Joe came home for the funeral.

Sitting in the living room of the Nimiroski home, I met a family coming to terms with a new national reality dawning on the entire nation just then, in 1965. I heard of Joe's anger and confusion. He had met jeering countrymen and women even then, even before massive protests in every part of the country. Americans had not yet shown how unwilling they were to accept automatically what their leaders were telling them – not about the length of their hair, not about the clothes they wore or the mind-altering drugs they were discovering or the music – or the war.

Joe stood on the other side of this upheaval. In his head, I learned, he'd been a Marine all his life. You fought for your country. There was no thought of finding reasons not to serve, of running to Canada, of conscientious objection.

In the beginning, the old script had sufficed. Joe said what every soldier said:

"I'll be back Mom. Of course, I'll be back. Don't worry so much. I've been well-trained."

And, he said, with a broad smile, "I have to come back for Valerie." His new wife, the sister of a friend, hadn't been a love interest. Just a friend. But then, home for his father's funeral -- surprising both of them in these years of accelerating time -- they became serious.

In a wedding-day picture, they seem to marvel at something neither expected, a love match, a marriage, the prospect of a future suddenly exciting, suddenly full of promise.

Photos at the wedding show Joe looking over his left shoulder, Valerie, behind him. In that moment, they seem to have willed the war out of their consciousness.

The reprieve couldn't last. He was back with his unit in less than a week. Two months later, he was dead.

Joe and Valerie had six days together. A six-day honeymoon. A six-day marriage.

For posting on Vietnam memorial survivors message board, Valerie said. "A beautiful man, a wonderful husband – for six days. I will miss you always."

20

General Assignment

Newspaper reporters enroll in life-long adult education courses.

C. Fraser Smith

I wondered if my story about Joe would get noticed. I thought I might have a head start on my colleagues since I had done so many feature obits.

I think my 1965 story may actually have prompted recognition in my new newsroom that this war would be more and more a part of the nation's life. It was one of those stories that inform editors of changing reality. It foreshadowed a decade of boy-next-door features. Eight other Marines from all over the country were killed in that same fight with Joe: Wichita, KS; Chappaqua, NY; Lexington, KY; Salinas, CA; Mountain View, CA among them.

It seems crass to say so now, but the story did accelerate my move into the city room. Most of us in the bureaus, if not all, wanted to be in the city. We wanted to be in a position to chronicle change already underway: racial struggles, women's rights, urban decay, illegal drug use, police brutality, characters – unreeling in front of us.

We heard of a young man trying to surrender after being accused of assaulting a police officer. Ideally, I would have been there to see and report the incident. I learned about it later and wrote an account based on what the parties told me.

"Two officials of the Providence antipoverty agency last night attempted to illuminate a bridge between the community and the ghetto." Increasingly, readers and newsrooms were interested in what happened between authorities – usually the police – and black people. Was it possible for a black man to turn himself in without being beaten? I had written about young men "transported" to the hospital for treatment of wounds suffered falling from a police vehicle, tripping on the curbing or the paddy wagon steps. The cops were at it again. And what could you do? You didn't see anything. You weren't there. All you had was the readily impeachable report of the accused. Who believed him or her?

In this case, Willie V. Perry, 22, was quietly – without tripping or falling – turning himself in during a peaceful meeting behind police headquarters. The police and the antipoverty agency were working together. That was news. Citizens, particularly in the black community, needed to know – not that some black man was arrested, but that it happened peacefully and that a new agency was working with police to make the peaceful unremarkable.

As I was moving up on the assignment chart – GA was above cops but below actual beats – a shift in perception was coming to newspapers. Younger, more socially conscious college graduate reporters were moving into newsrooms. Racial tensions were rising. Cities were in turmoil. School integration and dropout rates and drug addiction were becoming areas of intense concentration in the society – and, finally, in newsrooms.

Newspapers were starting to write more about the inner city – about poverty and a range of other issues hard-bitten newspaper types semi-sneered at. Are we becoming social workers? they asked. What happened yesterday was joined by why it happened and what anyone was doing about it.

Fires were also a GA staple. Typically, fires gave the inner city entre to the newspaper. Basketball might also trigger coverage. Run of the mill community life? Not so much. The 1967 Kerner Commission report on violence in cities said fires were the most common bits of inner city news. A Boston TV station signaled the change with an ad referencing Kerner: "It doesn't take a *fire* to get us into your neighborhood." Translation: We're interested in what's happening when there isn't a fire or a shooting or a break-in.

In truth, even fires weren't enough to assure what was automatic elsewhere in the city. We started covering fires under the same standards: were they seriously threatening to homes or businesses or firemen? The new standard gave an opportunity to showcase other issues: neglect, rent gouging, lead paint poisoning, dropout rates, welfare rates.

"The house at 66 Chester Street," I wrote one night, "is standing out of habit. Half its foundation is gone. Bricks have been poked out (and sold) by vandals who discovered that destruction can earn a few bucks."

We were suddenly writing more about the other half, how it lived. Evictions were as prevalent as fires. We tended to write about them on the East Side, off Hope Street where the middle class lived, not always on Prairie Avenue where poor black people lived.

"Bolts of water slammed into the top floor of the three-decker on Prairie Avenue, the major artery in the city's poorest neighborhood. A family of three was rescued suffering from smoke inhalation. One fireman was taken to nearby Rhode Island Hospital for treatment...."

I felt like I knew the house. I knew the neighborhood, filled with the typical Providence three-deckers. I'd been to night meetings at the community action agency's drop-in center just down the street, the only white guy in the room. I did a feature on the women with teacher's-aide jobs at the community school, hired to give them some employment – but more importantly to re-introduce families to schools, places where often they'd had bad experiences and therefore were not likely to insist on attendance with their own kids; a job training program from OIC – Opportunities Industrialization Center, founder Leon Sullivan. Michael Van Leesten, a tall black Providence man, ran that program, one of many established in those days to address the high rate of unemployment in black neighborhoods.

GA was leading me into a beat. I felt like I was inventing it. No such beat or responsibility existed, but the news, government action, and taxpayer money were pushing newspapers more deeply into new territory. Roughly defined eventually as poverty, the beat included the state welfare department; the new anti-poverty agency, Progress for Providence; and drug abuse. I became a kind of one-man news service for the downtrodden, producing story after story about every element of what we called the scourge of drugs, among other scourges. From marijuana on up, drugs were mysterious and frightening then, as if you could get addicted by being on the same street. Users themselves were frightening. They demanded attention.

I wrote about civil commitment – putting people in treatment against their will. The idea had some currency at the time. People were panicked. An extreme measure seemed reasonable then: Families were being torn apart by users who stole from their parents, or using their addiction and risk of a fatal overdose as leverage. The game usually involved costly legal representation and incarceration. There seemed to be no good alternative..

I went to a three-day seminar on drug abuse at Columbia University. Study trips like this were common in those days. Serious newspapers could invest in expertise for their reporters. Newspapers could be more authoritative if we knew what experts were working on. I'm not sure how much we learned. I remember being warned not to take the police figures on drug-arrest bounty too seriously: the seminar's view was that police loved to arrange piles of money and weapons on long tables to illustrate how effective they were. I think what they did and what we, the newspapers did, kept the fear factor stoked. Killer drugs that made police seem even more important in the city. They were defending us all. I think now these dog and pony shows were one of the first steps toward mass incarceration of black offenders. Civil commitment was part of the picture as well. I was for it initially because I had done a lot of reporting amid families driven to ruinous distraction by drug abuse.

A center of the Providence drug scene, I wrote, was known as The Junction, a 10-block northwest city area at Manton Avenue and various other streets. This focal point was an otherwise neat and tidy neighborhood north and west of downtown Providence. Gus Adair, a community worker, and a young parish priest were organizing drug abuse opposition from families, a couple of which had seen their sons die. I attended and wrote about several funerals, dramatizing the fear element in a way that seemed part of the story then – without, I fear, doing much to help anyone.

There were Junctions all over the state, state officials said. A certain mystery made the issue frightening. The arguments against grass – trumpeted by authority as a fearsome threshold drug that scared parents and lured new users.

21

Jack

What is a newspaperman? A peeper, an invader of privacy, a scandal peddler, a mischief-maker, a busybody, a man content to wear out his hams sitting in marble corridors waiting for important people to lie to him, a comic-strip intellectual, a human pomposity dilating on his constitutional duty, a drum thumper on a demagogue's bandwagon ...

Russell Baker, *The Good Times*

Hunter Thompson, referred to as a gonzo journalist after his dramatic approach to life in general, took a more biting turn:

...It's a damned shame that a field as potentially dynamic and vital as journalism should be overrun with dullards, bums, and hacks, hag-ridden with myopia, apathy, and complaisance, and generally stuck in a bog of stagnant mediocrity.

Thompson offered his dim view of us in a series of books including *Fear and Loathing in America: The Brutal Odyssey of an Outlaw Journalist.*

His brethren could have used some of his flair. But you might not have sent such a person to cover the zoning board. (It's also possible, I have to admit, that zoning issues would have won "best-read" accolades if the Gonzo man had been on the case.)

Newspaper writing was moving in his direction, though slowly. Slowly, in part, because we weren't parachuting in for stories the way he did. We lived in the communities we covered. We were going to be there the next day for the criticism or the bouquets.

The guys that came along with me had begun to evade the widely assumed and ultimately incapacitating handicap of booze -- another bit of the reporter's assumed reportorial trappings. The number of drunks seemed to fall as the job became more and more professionalized.

Of course, they weren't all gone.

I did this work long enough to be in the same Washington, D.C. newsroom as Jack Germond, whose capacity for food and drink was exceeded only by his skill as a political writer. I joined colleagues hiding in bathroom stalls at the end of the day lest we be recruited for an outing with the master. A night with Jack meant enough alcohol to wipe out the next day or so while the hangover receded. Never seemed to affect Germond. But, then, he was in practice.

Our model could be found in the family histories of men like my good friend and neighbor, Merrill Bailey. His parents had been newspaper people in Connecticut. His mother Bess in particular. She was a stringer for all the small Connecticut papers. Every newspaper person in the state knew her by her first name.

Merrill had wanted to go in another direction. (He may have suffered from inherited burnout.) He had a foreign relations master's degree from the University of Southern California to go with his Yale undergrad diploma. The State Department never called, so he hooked on with the *Journal*.

Spectacular colleagues joined us: Joe Day's father had been a Pulitzer Prize-winning editorial writer for the *Baltimore Sun*. Brian Dickinson had worked for the *New York Times* in some capacity that brought him into the ambit of the famous Scotty Reston, the *Times* columnist. Surely, he'd be off to New York any day.

The *Times* was actively courting Len Levin, an inside man of great newspaper acumen, a prototype keeper of high standards. Levin represented the sustaining human infrastructure of the *Providence Journal*. He chose not to leave.

We all worked for Jack Monaghan who ran the Providence afternoon paper, the *Evening Bulletin*. He had the requisite edgy focus of an old schooler augmented by the focus of a soccer goalie which he had been for Brown University.

Every morning he stalked the newsroom floor, foraging for stories.

"We have a paper to get out. Maybe you remember. "

Every reporter working that day took the question as if it were directed at him or her (not so much.) -- and it was.

"No," I would say, occasionally, lowering my head in the hope he would keep walking.

"That a firm no?" he would ask. I said yes often enough I could get away with no. But we lived in a what-have-you-done-for-me-lately world. On occasion, when the copy search failed, Jack's boss would suggest going back to our notes in search of something he referred to as "tight, light and bright" -- or "something cryptic. He meant concise, not mysterious. Duh.

Jack stayed on us. He knew we would never have as long as we wanted to "work" a story. We knew we might have to file something that would've been better with more time. He knew this as well as we did. But the paper had to come out.

His father had been editor of the *Pawtucket Times*, a paper of 44,000 circulation, well below the *Providence Journal's* number, about 150,000 when I was there. Having heard his father talk of every imaginable newspaper issue -- and working there as a teenaged copy kid -- he had more knowledge of the job and the culture of newspapers than most of us, new or veteran. Jack was a representative of that group of newspaper people that gave journalism generation after generation of practitioners born to the job. There was a kind of built-in replenishment.

And there was also the newsroom, itself a classroom.

"Everything I know I learned from a guy named Eddie Murphy, a WWII vet. I sat next to him. I sat beside him and every day I learned. We talked about the stories of that day. We talked about being a reporter, what you could do, you couldn't do." You couldn't let your own thoughts and predilections into the story. interview interesting people. You couldn't invent quotes. Obvious but worth hearing.

Monaghan liked the license, the entre reporters were granted. You could go in and talk to governors and mayors. It made you think you could do something useful, something important.

He had an early taste of the political world as well. (Many if not all editors had been on the street. They had covered the beats. The system thereby reinforced itself and provided a path upward if you wanted to go that way. It made newspapers one of those self-sufficient organizations. People learned the work —and the ethical guidelines. (Where will that schooling come from in the future?)

On one election day, as a "runner," he ferried information – turnout estimates, voting machine problems, if any -- from polling places to the city desk. In addition to the various candidate races that year, voters were being asked to approve changes to the city charter, the basic rules of running government. Democrats, who knew the existing rules by heart, opposed changes that would remove their advantage at least for a while.

One of the polling places was across from the Democratic Party wardroom or headquarters on Pawtucket Avenue. The party had managed to be located near what mattered most to them.

After the polls closed, city police took the paper ballots to city hall. But maybe not directly to city hall, not on this night at least.

Young Jack followed the cops out of the board of election office and watched them walk to the Democratic wardroom, a blatant, outrageous hijacking. Through a window, he watched party men replace some of the ballots with new ones marked No on the charter question.

The editor's son reported what he had seen. The stakes were high. The city's governing document might be affected. But what he saw could go no further. He was just a high school kid. If you were going to report something seriously corrupt, your reporter had to be a reporter, a professional.

As it turned out, the charter changes were approved. And the Democrats were spared embarrassment or worse.

Monaghan was in the reporter's fold before this excitement.

After Brown, he worked seven years for his father's paper before getting hired by the *Journal*. He covered some of the early years of the War on Poverty aggressively enough to become a prime irritant to Sargent Shriver, a Kennedy family member and the program's national director. Shriver tried to hire Monaghan -- a compliment to be sure. For Shriver, it may have been a two-fer. He'd get a good PR guy and he'd lose an annoying reporter who was asking the right questions. That sort of re-emptive approach happened often as some reporters left for the higher wages in private public jobs.

Jack declined. He had a young family and no interest in moving to Washington, D.C.

All the while, life in the newsroom – as in the rest of society – was changing. The newspaper needed black reporters, so Monaghan and the *Journal's* only black reporter toured the country looking for good black reporters.

"The *Times* was always there first, so the people we wanted we couldn't get," he said.

For me and others on the paper, Monaghan earned a career award during one of the newspaper's days of ignominy. The paper decided to invest in the refurbishment of the city's premier hotel, the Biltmore, across the street from City Hall and down the shallow hill from the rail station.

When the work was done, the editors sent one of the paper's columnists, Tony Lioce, to write a feature.

"Really nice," he wrote, "but bring your checkbook."

The managers of the newspaper were not amused. They ordered a punishment: Lioce would no longer have a column and he was forthwith re-assigned to the Newport bureau. This was not the worst place in the world to work, but it was a clear demotion. In truth, it hurt the paper more than Lioce. His prose enlivened every offering, gave it reach beyond the straight-ahead newspaper style. (He was a bit closer to Hunter Thompson model.)

Pretty embarrassing – if publisher types could be embarrassed. Their editors, including Monaghan, had edited the story and put it in the newspaper. (Some of them would have enjoyed a Newport punishment.)

Monaghan thought he was dealing with a columnist, a writer with the columnist's license to write with flare. Apparently, they thought Lioce would know what they wanted or didn't want. Maybe he did but until then he thought his newspaper wanted columnists to exercise their mandate. It was not the first time they would display their misunderstanding of their newspaper's role.

Jack defended the column, defended Lioce and upheld the newspaper's professionalism. He found himself in a certain degree of bad odor with ownership for a time – for doing his job. Not a happy story, but one that showed principle could survive, if not cleanly. Monaghan got "stand-up" cred.

22

The Role of Women

When Cory Dean came down the hill from Brown to the *Journal* she found anti-women bias fading – slowly. She was among younger reporters chosen for a trial run on the city desk. By all accounts, she did well. Al Johnson, the city editor, praised her work.

Well, she said, do you think I might be considered for any opening on your staff?

Johnson frowned.

We already have a woman, he said.

Reporting wasn't hand-to-hand combat unless you were a woman trying to get hired by a paper in the 1950s or '60s. You didn't need a lot of upper body strength.

Foul reporter language offending female ears wasn't an issue. Contrary, that is, to one of the excuses for maintaining a woman-free newsroom. Suzanne Wooton, a female editor of mine, as good or better than any editor I ever had achieved fame by inventing her own alphabet. She went beyond the familiar way of answering a question in the exclamatory affirmative:

"Are you really going to do that?"

"Fucking A!"

She didn't stop there. Her alphabet went on, when necessary, to " "Fucking B, Fucking C," etc.

The woman reporter at the *Journal* when I arrived was Carol Young, the education writer, a graduate of the journalism school at Syracuse University and a committed workaholic. She remembered an introductory meeting when she arrived – with a roomful of men, 25 or so. No women.

If there was anti-woman bias at the *Journal,* Carol just ignored it. At one of those occasional "meet the editors" sessions, a questioner in the audience asked, "What's the role of women at the *Journal?*"

"No role at all," came the answer.

"No, I'm serious," she said.

"I am too," came the answer. There followed a recitation of the usual lame commentaries.

When Carol started out-working everyone in the room, the issue became a non-issue. Editors started saying they only wanted to know you could do the work.

One of my very progressive friends, Irwin Becker, resented her – but not for taking a man's job. Once when she was looking for something in a desk drawer and Irwin was standing nearby, he could see a pile of uncashed paychecks. Weeks and weeks of them, it seemed. She didn't have a family as he did. And, she was too busy to go to the bank. The rest of us, including Irwin—we'd have been in line for payday loans. Checks did not lie around in our desks.

So quota or not, the ProJo had two women, Carol and Cory, at the same time.

I met Cory one night at a community meeting on Prairie Avenue in the heart of black Providence. She was still at Brown then, but covering the city as a reporter for the *Brown Daily Herald,* the campus newspaper. She applied to the *Journal,* moved quickly through suburban office assignments and became an assistant editor.

I began to hear that Cory Dean was, as they said in the news trade, "good." It meant better than good. It meant special, exceptionally competent. The good word on Cory got out in the broader newspaper world.

My friend Ham Davis, the *Journal's* political reporter, one of the boys Tim Crouse wrote about it in his 1973 presidential campaign epic, *The Boys on the Bus.* Davis saw how good she was and told his friends. One of them, a *New York Times* man, decided to check it out,

Would she come to New York for an interview?

Cory said no. Not interested. I was surprised but not that surprised. She had what she wanted. She had a keen eye for the world she lived in. She loved language and yearned for the ocean, for the nearby Horseneck Beach, for the Narragansett Bay and for everything about living near the water. We thought for years, that the newspaper's managers tried to explain why we weren't getting a raise by throwing the ocean into the mix.

You're so lucky. It's a treat to live near the Atlantic – as if the publisher had arranged to locate his paper near the beach just for us. I'm sure Cory nodded appreciatively.

Eventually and then regularly, more calls from New York.

"Don't waste your time," she would say in words to that effect.

I'm hearing all of this with a mixture of envy and disbelief.

She's saying no to the *Times?* Really? Over and over actually.

"No" seemed to make the envoys even more determined.

One suitor insisted on flying up for lunch. Okay, she said, thinking to herself, I warned you. She made a lunch reservation in a restaurant where she could see the water as she and her guest talked. The water, the ocean. You won't be able to see the ocean from Times Square, she said to herself.

Still the newspaper persisted – and finally she agreed to go for a tryout on the copy desk. She went, she conceded later, because the *Times* would pay her about a thousand dollars for the week, way more than the *Journal* was paying then – and enough to buy a set of Barcelona chairs, knockoffs of chairs made by the architect Mies van der Rohe.

Still having no interest at all in living in New York, she was free, she thought, to say exactly what she thought of the *Times'* operation. She could, that is, be interviewing them and the work they did. One morning, she and her mates looked over a story filed by one of the paper's better known writers, an expert on military affairs. There was no discernible news in the piece.

"Spike it," she said.

The piece reminded her of a singular sort of *Providence Journal* story from the suburbs. In lore, such stories carried the name of the writer – or, you might say, perpetrator. A "sturgeon," for example. These were stories of little to no merit sometimes filed to fill space or and to represent that suburban office's expected daily offering.

The writer would return to his office and engage in a "brain dump," a typescript of virtually everything the official had said. Stories of this sort were called by the perpetrator's name,

So, she said without hesitating, "Spike this." Was there any risk here? Why did she feel she could deal with what was called "live copy" – a story headed for the publication in the paper as worthless? The idea was to see how the prospect would deal with such stories once hired.

Maybe it was a test. If you weren't willing to challenge the stars, you might not make it on the *Times* desk. Was she brave? Or was it a risk-free move, since she made clear she had no interest in the job.

She was channeling Don Smith, the editor she worked for in Providence, one reason no one could hire her away. She knew Smith would have nodded affirmatively when she employed the spike. (Perhaps it is important to say real spikes were the tool of choice then for killing stories.)

Davis heard she had delivered one of the best tryouts in *Times* history.

Still she said no.

Some years later, unhappy with some offence, she called the *Times* recruiter.

"Offer still open?"

"Oh, yeah."

After a few years on the Science desk she became its editor. She wrote a book, *Against the Tide*, about corrosive shore development, eroding beaches and the oceans. She later retired to teach at Brown, where she shows young people how to tell the difference between a real news story and a sturgeon.

What she taught me was the difference between a plan and a life. A representative of the *Times* and I had that single meeting eons ago. I had found my good paper, the *Sun*. (I got over my *Times* obsession. I would have gone to work there, of course, but I no longer "yearned tragically" to be there as Cory would have put it.) the *Washington Post* called me several times, but

I never got past the second or third bank of interviewing editors. After a few years, I got a Sunday column at Mencken's newspaper. He actually wrote for the *Evening Sun*, but he was part of the overall operation, morning and evening. Close enough.

23

Are You Neck'st?

I have found it easier to identify with the characters who verge upon hysteria ... But these seemingly fragile people are the strong people really.

Tennessee Williams

The Puritan Roger Williams came to Rhode Island from an intolerant Massachusetts. He and the other state's founders might have called it the Hope State, drawing on the quest for religious freedom and a better life in general. Reality led to Ocean State. Before manufacturing, Rhode Islanders made their living in and around the sea.

Nevertheless, "Hope" showed up everywhere: on banks, on dry cleaning shops and on one important street sign. Hope, a major tributary connected most of the city's east side. Everyone, it seemed, lived "off Hope," not hope, itself, but Hope, the street. (The Target of its time was called Ann and Hope's.)

Hope became short-hand for giving directions in the city. Brown University, the Rhode Island Reds hockey arena and Wayland Square's shops were, more or less, "off Hope."

Fox Point was more or less "off Hope." I drove over there one Saturday, looking for a hardware store – and buying my newly discovered Cape Verdean donut and looking for stories. I was always working.

I noticed a hand-lettered sign in front of the junk store at 312 South Main Street challenged passersby:

"Are you neck'st?"

If you didn't know Sam Corrado's story, if you didn't get his joke, a pillory, with the usual holes for head and hands, stood nearby.

A holiday message, nailed to the front door announced:

"We have already been evicted. May all of you have a Merry Christmas. God Bless."

Sam Corrado, sign-maker and author of holiday greetings, had been fighting City Hall for four years. The city's Redevelopment Authority was evicting him even before his legal protest had been concluded. Christmas, 1967, was two days away.

With the exception of his friend, Jim Kane and me that day, the junkman fought alone. In a later time, he might have become a folk hero. Community organizers, who would have their day in the 1970s and '80s, were always on the lookout for a cause and someone to lead it. People might have marched in front of his building. On the other hand, he was a bit of a loner and might have rejected help.

He thought people would respond to his singular battle. Jim Kane and a few others did. Kane drove up as Corrado's shop was being dismantled, his faded green station wagon pulling to the curb behind one of the moving vans.

"I didn't know they can move a man out of his own building," Kane said.

They could. They could "take" Corrado's used furniture store because it stood in the way of a big-money, out-of-towner's renewal project. The laws of eminent domain would prevail over a cranky, obsessed local who thought he had rights. What about the little man? He kept asking.

What about *my* domain?

I got his questions into the newspapers. I worked for both: the *Journal* in the morning, the *Evening Bulletin* in the afternoon. I wanted to stand up for him. He had nerve and he was pushing all the Constitutional buttons. He had gone to court on his own nickel. He invoked the processes that in theory protect all our "necks." He was raising uncomfortable questions. Who was protected by the Constitution? The kind of story newspapers had to cover. Who would if we didn't?

Call him a crank. He was. But cranks, as Tennessee suggests, were the strong people. They make us think when we think we are too busy to think. What was the city doing here – and everywhere it used its power to "take" your property. Sam always called the building his "historic private property."

Maybe there was something of a prurient interest in stories about cranks, but often the public interest was invoked – as it was here – to mask something done for the wealthy and powerful.

Corrado, of course, was neither. He could be seen, outside his store, working on the legal papers himself.

"Urban renewal is coming," he all but shouted. "Urban renewal is coming." The law was the law but officials were running amok, he said.

He was a showman. He was clever with words. I'm sure he reveled in the small spectacle he created. He was a victim with a cause. His Paul Revere-like warning was, nevertheless, unheard for the most part.

The lack of a movement spurred him. He did not relent.

Nor did he find much sympathy on the newspaper's editorial page. My friend, Brian, thought Sam should get out of the way. His street, not far from downtown, needed new life. The city had plans. An eminent domain proceeding was perfectly fine – in place precisely to deal with unreasonable opposition.

But what of Sam's plans? He wanted to be part of the bright new cityscape, the new apartments and law offices and carriage trade shops he knew would be coming. The Providence River, Brown University and the Rhode Island School of Design were his neighbors. All the elements were in place. But the renaissance that would follow would be for others. Sam could see it. He could see a South Main that did not include him. He said it over and over as well. The rest of the city, I am guessing, said cynically, "He's right, but what can you do?"

And now, just before Christmas, 1967, the Providence County sheriff and a crew, King Moving and Storage, were hauling load after load of his dusty exotic wares to trucks on the street. The sheriff and his men ratified Corrado's junk store advertising boast: there were at least a million items, as his sign promised.

A secondhand store license hung from a nearby rafter next to a single boxing glove and a picture of Snoopy the Peanuts star. "I wish urban renewal was a fire hydrant," Snoopy was saying.

"Hey Corrado," said a sign over head, "I've been waiting 39 years for a secondhand store that could save me money." Jack Benny, the famous skinflint, was the alleged author. Benny had never been there.

A grinding rip cried out as the store's main display case fell. Jim Kane flinched. Soon there was only a wood burning stove in the front of the building. Workers warmed themselves.

Money was an issue in Corrado's campaign, to be sure. How much would he get for the building and the business it housed?

"You couldn't buy a bicycle for the money they want to give him," Kane said.

Corrado cared more about due process, equal protection of the laws and property rights. The building, he said, was 'his precious, private, historic property." He spent many years of his life on this project.

Eventually, no other options available, he settled for about $50,000.

24

Hair Shirt

Stocker let his arms collapse into his lap, not letting go of the newspaper which he had been holding at arm's length and eye level. He stared off into the middle distance, his expression a mix of impatience and exasperation.

I turned toward him, assuming he had invited a question. The crumpling paper was a signal. I didn't say anything. He out-waited me.

"What?" I said finally.

"Our paper calls this column *In Perspective*," he said with disdain, dipping his head toward the paper in his lap. "Usually it has about this much perspective," he said lifting it out of his lap and holding it an inch or two from his face.

Eliot Stocker, with his perfect military style crew cut and his precisely trimmed mustache – as white and translucent as his hair – served as the newspaper's chief, unofficial scold. Every newspaper had to have a hair shirt, an irritating presence, he said. He had elected himself.

In Perspective was a staff-written feature that ran on the op-ed page, a place of awe-inspiring importance to me. I wanted to be on that page. The pieces were laid out so beautifully. Often there was art – a photo or a drawing. *In Perspective* ran down the full length of the page, almost always in the righthand column. These pieces were what some editors called "slices of life" – slices of the writer's life. Ideally, there would be a slant – a perspective on some quirky commonplace. The writers were reporters or editors on the *Journal,* and so the submissions offered slices of Providence or Rhode Island life. (The term had become a cliché describing a good angle on something interesting, if done well with perspective, but not newsy.) The bylines were the writer's initials and so, in a sense, they were written by us to us. Maybe regular readers knew who had done the work. *We* all knew, of course. We knew our colleagues knew. Al Johnson, the timid-seeming city editor, wrote these pieces with regularity. I wanted to be good at everything, but I think *In Perspective* became my goal – even more eventually than working for the *Times* – (easy you might say since the *Times* was not calling).

Elsewhere on the page were the national or international thinkers and stylists. To be in their company for a day was a moment of pride for me and the other new guys, the young new guys. You were showing what you could do all on your own. It was also a chance to show what you couldn't do. Stocker made himself available for that chore.

He was the tribune of failure, a man who thought someone had to point it out – not because he wanted to humiliate but to rail against anything that made the newspaper look less than discerning and smart. He was a curmudgeon of course but also a keeper of standards.

To put it another way, he was an arbiter of quality. Was the piece funny? Was it insightful? Was it illuminating? Was there any discernible perspective? Or was there no more perspective than you got with the newspaper an inch or so in front of your face? Too often, he thought, the answer was "no". So he had to say something. He couldn't help himself. Here we had another dimension of the newsroom's self-policing system. (Usually the offender was not nearby.) This was the newsroom as J-school.

Elliott Stocker was a kind of free-floating truth teller in the land of people who had, even if unstated, a fairly high opinion of themselves. *In Perspective* was an outlet for the creative impulse that was *verboten* in almost every other part of the paper – which in those days worshiped at the Altar of Straight Ahead, the unswerving presentation of news. Things were changing in newsrooms, but they had not really changed.

The newspaper anchored, stabilized and delivered. You could count on it.

I thought of *In Perspective* as a try-out space. If you could handle these pieces you might have other potential. Maybe you belonged in Features. Or if there was a story that demanded a light touch, or a story that cried out for perspective in the news columns – or if irony was needed or the deft handling of difficult or sensitive material – he (again, almost never she in those days) might be discovered on the op-ed page. If the writing wasn't always worthy – with that soupcon of perspective missing, well, it was serving its purpose by weeding out the merely ambitious.

Elliott's presence could not be missed. Poor word usage offended him as much as lack of perspective in *In Perspective*. He railed against periphrasis – the unnecessary qualifier. I think he enjoyed saying the word and defining it for people – like me – who had never heard of it:

"The distraught man leapt from the bridge into the water – below," he would say, drawing out his pronunciation of "below." "What should we be saying: 'The man jumped from the bridge into the water – above?'" then often he would add: "Does anyone read this paper before they print it?"

I took his point. Looking back, I realize that every one of these mini-tantrums was a lesson. Not necessarily a correction, but something to be held onto for a career, a part of the process of learning – accuracy, precision and clean writing. This is what happened in newsrooms. This is what we lose without them.

25

Vultures

Stocker had been city editor of a paper in Worcester, Massachusetts, just north of Providence. He'd been a reporter there. And then an editor. I didn't know why he was back on "the floor" with the rest of us. I did know he was a taskmaster.

He had interesting, poignant, instructive stories from his reporting life. Once, while covering cops, he'd heard on the police scanner a report of twin boys falling through ice in a pond and drowning.

He knew what his desk (aka his editor) would want. He knew what he had to do even as his dread all but overcame him. He'd have to speak with the parents -- get a photograph. Most of all, (shades of "da Joisey") a photograph of the twins. Do I really want to keep doing this, he thought, as he headed for the door.

He drove to the boys' home and was about to knock on the door when, out of the corner of his eye, he saw a police cruiser pull up. He thought he knew what that meant: The parents didn't know what had happened.

He turned and walked back down to the street. He would wait for the police to tell them. Sometimes being quick out of the box didn't serve well – not you, not the newspaper. He wondered years later whether it was necessary to ask husbands or wives or the parents of twins if they had a photograph of the departed. It was necessary. But it was possible to ask during a conversation about the deceased when the request would seem natural and even welcome.

I hated these moments, too. I never got used to them – but I also saw the role I played in the lives of families and communities. My own way of getting past it was to become the parents in my mind. In my game with myself I was both the giver and receiver of the news. I felt the pain. The worst of it would go away for me. I knew it would never end for the people I was speaking to about their killed-in-action son or accident victim son or their murdered daughter. It would not be the acute pain but it would last as it had with Stocker. He would never forget what happened as he caught himself just before knocking. Here was the stuff of emotional callus, the moments that erode empathy. I asked myself then and later if I had saved a corner of my concern for others as I stayed in a profession that sent me to such places over and over. Much of the cynical stuff you may have heard about how reporters behave was protective. You might see more of it in the people who cared and hurt sympathetically most. The other saving aspect of it all was avoiding too much – visible – concern. Grieving parties did not need someone else falling apart. Businesslike was the preferred mien.

At some point, I realized too that there was something immediately useful in what we did. The newspaper would report on the death of twin boys. Neighbors would see and respond. School teachers and principals would be alerted. Friends would read and come by with casseroles. By the time some people knocked on the door, people had read my story and seen the picture we had to have. We were not wallowing in loss. We were summoning community.

These wrenching tragedies were dramatic and rare – which of course made them news. But they were less rare in the life of a newspaper. You had to deal with them there even if it made you look like a vulture. (Newspaper critics used that word.) The people you met at these moments were, eventually, appreciative if you worked at handling the tough stories with feeling. After 241 Marines were killed in October, 1983, during the bombing of a barracks in Beirut, I wrote a magazine story about one of the casualties. People were grateful, happy to have a record of that life, happy that others knew what had been treasured and then honored in the wider community.

26

Rita

On slow days, at least, there was lunch. Lunch at Paul's. Bacon cheese burgers beckoned – and Rita, the waitress.

"The usual," I'd say. She always wrote it down. I had been having the same thing for months. She wrote with a kind of resentful speed. We had given her orders, certifying her place in the equation. She would have to serve us.

I would order tea as well so she would return periodically with a pot of hot water.

"Water your bag?" she asked. It was her favorite moment any time we landed at Paul's.

"Thanks," I would say. Brian would look up as if the skanky undertone offended him. It probably did, actually. Merrill would smile. Maybe there would be a giggle, suppressed a bit, but audible. Every time she said it and she said it every time. The giggle would please her, it seemed, as if she had proved once again the haughty reporters were open to a little off-color parry and thrust, in spite of our self-important selves.

She was all legs, it seemed, two narrow limbs stuck into a short, formless body. She looked a bit afflicted by long-time exposure to smoke and alcohol. Her voice had a bit of the barroom burr. With her offer to refill the teacup, she would complete a presentation of self as just a bit party-worn and open to censure. She seemed to invite a form of scorn. Of course, sometimes we would laugh and she would smile as she delivered the warm-up.

This was the routine at Paul's. It was just around the corner from Hope's, a bar we often patronized on an alley across the street from the *Journal's* front door. You didn't dine there. It was a beer place. A copy editor or two was known to sleep there on one of the shuffle board tables.

For variety, we occasionally headed for the Greyhound Bus station behind the *Journal* building. We'd spot some of the brass over there, one of the vice presidents or an assistant to the publisher.

We didn't like them much. After the strike in 1968, one of them talked about pruning the tree, making sure I heard.

The bus station had a leavening effect. The suits all graduated from Harvard or the Wharton School. Seemed like a come-down for them. They couldn't always be dining at the Hope Club, (the publisher's hangout.) I wondered if any of them ever had his bag watered by Rita.

I wrote an *In Perspective* column about her. Perspective was built-in I thought.

27

Hartford Park

In 1968, I moved with my wife and 3-year-old daughter into an 11-story public housing project high rise. It had been shuttered and closed off in chain link fencing – a harsh symbol of well-intentioned public policy failure.

The project's most prominent feature was the building of three-bedroom apartments. That's where we moved with a class of 15 or so 18-year-old college students. The building, known as Number 2 or simply Two, had become toxic. Teenagers, in and out of correction facilities, used it as jungle gym. They stole and sniffed glue and terrorized families without trying to, just being there, a looming threat. Government hated to give up on a big investment even though its experiment with troubled families living on top of each other in tall buildings had long since been a failure. The building tended to warn people away year after year.

I convinced my adventurous and open-minded wife that we would be safe behind the chain links that kept miscreants out– and that we might – *I* might – get a pretty good story out of it. We moved from Larch Street off Hope to a neighborhood where many had lost hope.

The news value? Providence had 400 vacancies in its public housing inventory, even as the city needed more low-income housing. It was not a unique failure. New Haven, Bridgeport, Buffalo and many other cities had similar situations. The buildings became near traps. Families there didn't have money to move.

Maybe our stay and my reporting would have national significance. And, we would be part of what the college called an urban laboratory.

At the end of the year, I wrote a three-part series.

I began with a travel guide from downtown Providence to the projects as if people were dying to get there.

"Watch the clerks and the hairdressers and others from the workaday world line up against the plate glass store windows. Listen to the orations of the drunks. Watch the slow-gaited dudes in their bright ensembles and the sailors and the 'fancy ladies.' Wait for the Number 28 bus, Hartford Avenue.

"Ride past giant, pastel shaded stuffed animals in the window of an Olneyville Square shop and start to get your change ready.

"Get out at the corner of Bodell Avenue and begin to feel the aura of Hartford Park, a public housing project. Walk past the towering quarters for the elderly on Whelan Road and see the macadam rear yards sequined with shattered soda bottles. See the children, barefooted, cartwheeling through it.

"You are in the 'progicks' – where Uncle Sam is the absentee landlord, where social service types search for 'community,' where the results of a 15-year-old experiment in 'democratic living' – the words are from the tenants' manual – have been known and ignored for too long.

"'Democratic living' at Hartford Park does mean equality. It means when one child is attacked by a drug addict, parents of all other children must be equally fearful. It means that when one teenager sniffs glue or robs a store, all the others are judged equally guilty of sniffing and stealing.

"… It means that any foul word scribbled on any building was scribbled by you and that all garbage and glass and litter was left by you. It means that everyone is equally undesirable as a prospective tenant anywhere else simply because they live there now."

The projects were meant to be temporary, way stations on the way to the suburbs or to better housing in the city. Officials called it "transitional housing." There were Korean War vets in particular looking for places to live in a then-tight housing market.

The project manager, "Father" Hynes seemed as trapped as his tenants. Affable, always smiling, he had succinct advice for beleaguered families: Get out.

"I get after many of the families. I tell them there is another way of life," he said. I wonder, looking back, if these urgings didn't reinforce the fear that, since they had been unable to move on, they were trapped. Some people said they deliberately refused to meet their neighbors. They would then have unwanted attachments – not a recipe for community and neighborhood.

Some of the problem was imbedded in the initial thinking: Build housing cheaply. The need was temporary – (until it became permanent). The buildings looked brutally dull and hard-edged. I still remember my daughter falling one day. She seemed to bounce off the cinder-block walls and concrete floor. What had I gotten us into? Fortunately, she was unhurt.

At least I knew we could – would – move out in time. The people we met had similar hopes.

I dropped in on a man and a woman one night and found them poring over ads for housing.

"Are you planning to move?" I asked.

"Yes, we are," the man said.

"How long have you been looking?" I asked.

"Since we moved in," the woman said. It was 1966. She came to Hartford Park in 1954, the year the project opened.

Young people had no better luck – and often made their prospects worse.

In my series, I wrote about a group of teenagers and young adults, one in particular.

"At 24 he clings to an image of himself as a wily bird of prey, tough when cornered, fleet of foot and mind, a generous modern-day Robin Hood.

"He is a celebrity at Hartford Park, though not universally admired. Violence mars the popular notion of his character – stories of guns and "pipings" (lengths of pipe were a weapon of choice, employed without restraint in fights) in which the enemy is taught a lesson.

"When he was younger he wanted to become a legend. To many, he has become the archetype of a way of life, a romantically realistic way of facing the world. He is copied frequently and, one suspects, the style of the copiers does a disservice to whatever good may be found in the original...."

"...He knows every dimpled surface of every concrete building. Part of his reputation has been absorbed by 2 Whelan Road... He can be seen as the resident gymnast, performing escapes Houdini might have been proud of..."

He left Providence for a while, jumping bail and doing a couple nickel and dime robberies. He applied for work at a chemical company. His aptitude test scores were high.

He was offered a job.

"Can you be bonded?" he was asked.

Yes, he said, having no alternative. An investigation uncovered the truth.

He was proud of the test scores – about all he got from the experience.

At home, at Hartford Park, he defended his way of life: "There's no excuse for stealing," he starts. "When I steal I know I'm a thief. My only defense is that I only take from people who can afford it..." I tried to address that rationale in the series:

"Of course, this way of life did not begin with him. He is simply one of its more intelligent and handsome proponents. And because he is these things, he is also one of its most tragic victims."

Joe Ungaro, my editor, told me the series, nominated by the *Journal*, was considered for a Pulitzer Prize,

I remember exactly what he said.

"Don't get your hopes raised too high." So of course, I walked away with my hopes leaping through the ceiling. I couldn't think of anything else for the next two months.

My wife brought me back to reality, or tried to. I was too young for a Pulitzer Prize, she reasoned.

I had no such concern.

At any rate, I didn't win.

I tried to learn from the experience. I think I got as far as I had because we had done a dramatic thing – moving into a public housing project. Who does that? Some of what I reported was pretty good, illuminating the public policy issues: why so many families found "the projicks" corrosive, how they stigmatized everyone who lived in them and the need for a kind of human rehabilitation.

I had a lot more to learn, to be sure. My wife was right about that. Of course, had I won, my youth would have made the prize even sweeter.

At about this time, I think, my very good friend Ham Davis gave me a final bit of leavening counsel:

"You know the prize you get?" he said. "It's when they put your stuff in the newspaper. Isn't that why you wanted to be a reporter?"

He was right. And one of these days I will fully accept it.

28

Low-Hanging Fruit

Meanwhile, the new face of democracy inevitably involved unforeseen problems.

Dickie Callei and his pal, Joey "One-Arm" Tomasso, -- two second or third rate thugs -- must have looked at the community action agency, Progress for Providence, as low hanging fruit.

Wasn't their Federal Hill neighborhood a community?

Didn't it have poverty?

Didn't Dickie and Joey love action?

Hadn't they been excluded from the seats of power? (For generations, Providence had been run by Larry McGarry and other born-canny Irish.)

The federal poverty war planners left the door open for Dickie and Joey, enforcers with delusions of rank and authority. They walked into the community action program with takeover on their minds.

Callei went a step further. He assumed the role of back-up to Raymond L.S. Patriarca, identified by the FBI as New England's crime boss. Raymond was in jail when the poverty/community action program came to town. He might have been a bit startled by this opportunity. He and his community were entitled to services and ideas. It didn't involve any form of theft or political influence. If you were a community you were in.

To understate the matter, Joey and Dickie were not what President Johnson's men had in mind when they called for "maximum feasible participation of the poor." Surely Washington didn't expect members of known crime families to take over the programs. Sometimes the locals actually knew things Washington didn't.

The Progress for Providence director, Cleo Lachapelle, loved the idea of an attack on the Democratic political bosses, including the idea that the Establishment would pay for it. The 6-foot-6 Lachapelle had been working on youth diversion programs for several years. Senator Abraham Ribicoff of Connecticut had learned a lot about how these programs work. They were the front rank of Johnson's effort. His poverty war was not brand new. He and Lachapelle and other local program directors had been on the case long before Johnson's program.

Lachapelle knew bad news when he saw and heard it. Dickie and Joey for example. The program was obliged by law to welcome them. A criminal record alone did not disqualify anyone from serving in the war on poverty and its democratic subplots. Poor people often had criminal records, not always deserved. That was sort of the point. In its parallel governing system, the rules could be loosened.

Episodes like this made some of us laugh. There were a lot of Joey and Dickie incidents, and only one Lachapelle to absorb and deflect all the fallout.

"There goes Cleo," someone said, "hanging ten on a wave of shit." He had patience. He was a stoic, a good talker and an equally good listener.

Dickie and Joey, mob-tainted activists, emerged suddenly with a patina of respectability.

They couldn't sustain it.

They held PforP community meetings in a house next to the Old Canteen, a restaurant thought to be a hangout for the Mob. They sent various worthies to the PforP offices in search of jobs. Dickie and Joey became a government-sponsored job referral agency.

By this time, the war on poverty and the welfare rights movement were my beats. I don't recall writing a word about Dickie and Joey until one night someone was murdered outside their anti-poverty office on Federal Hill. The intended target had been making a nuisance of himself, disrupting the meeting, challenging the leadership.

Neighborhood meetings were inevitably disruptive. People were not experts in Robert's Rules. There tended to be a lot of shouting. Refusing to take orders was healthy – up to a point. Dickie Callei and Joey didn't get the memo. For them, opposition was intolerable.

So suddenly a serial disrupter tried to get the floor one more time.

"That was the coop de grace," someone at the meeting reported later. He said "coup" as if it were the word for chicken house. The story was that Joey had done the shooting – and because his eyesight was poor, killed the wrong guy -- the gang that literally couldn't shoot straight. Someone just walking by got the bullet instead of the nuisance.

Meanwhile, as the program tried to build new citizens, the politically entrenched variety were climbing back into the game.

Chicago's Richard Daley, who had promised to help President Johnson with the program, quickly realized he was under attack by the poverty warriors who had federal money on their side. Johnson had promised Daley the "wherewithal."

When it didn't arrive, he enlisted the help of a well-regarded Oregon representative, Edith Green, then at work on public education issues. She agreed to attach amendments to a bill, shifting the money to Daley and other mayors.

Johnson was, by then, more than ever preoccupied by the war in Southeast Asia. His boast that Americans could have guns and butter was looking empty. His domestic war generals were reportedly advised that the battle would have to be waged on the cheap.

But the poverty war was not over. It had a broader base than possibly Daley understood. Those who found the war ill-conceived failed to see the effect of the Kennedy/Johnson/Harrington demand for a multi-front war. They failed to account for a team of young lawyers on board to provide backup seldom available to the poor.

John Roney and his Providence team of Legal Services lawyers were revolutionaries. These young, aggressive advocates enlisted in the war with no idea what they could and couldn't do. They eagerly confronted bureaucrats who turned out to be incapable defenders of mindless rules.

On a wall in his downtown Providence office, Roney had a quote from Albert Camus, the French writer and philosopher.

"I would love my country more if I did not love justice."

Justice as well as jobs had been an objective of Johnson's war. All of this – the lawyers, the organizers and the newly inspired poor – added up to a revolution.

Roney did almost daily battle with the Rhode Island welfare bureaucrats and their suddenly beleaguered lawyers. One class action lawsuit forced the state to honor federal law providing basic household furniture to welfare moms who suddenly had something to organize around. Until Johnson's war, until Legal Services, until the National Welfare Rights Organization, many recipients had no idea what the law allowed. A lot of these anti-poverty initiatives succeeded by spreading information -- and expertise.

Some allowances had been intended for "residual" welfare recipients, the few remaining recipients on the rolls after most found jobs and started making it on their own. That was the theory.

The states yelped in fiscal pain. Demands for "kitchen sets," withheld though allowed by law, were leading to state bankruptcy.

In court, Roney argued that the law was the law. Remove the allowances from the law or comply with it. Judge Raymond J. Pettine quickly accepted Roney's position, brushing aside the state's empty arguments. The assistant Rhode Island attorney general sent to argue a losing case was treated like a pampered Establishment bureaucrat who had never been required to understand and defend the law -- and who didn't realize his cause was lost. He was humiliated -- trounced by Roney and a judge who seemed to enjoy the other guy's pain.

Without legal services, welfare recipients wouldn't have gotten into court at all.

29

Odd Couple

One day the mobbed-up Callei walked into the newsroom, past me to a spot in front of the city editor. I recognized him from his antipoverty program exploits with Joey.

Callei began to rant.

"Where's fucking Becker?

"I'm gonna' kick the shit out of him."

He seemed to have enough anger to work his way through the whole room.

Energy and extraordinary backing. He'd come with his lawyer, Joe Bevilacqua, a member of the Rhode Island House of Representatives.

My friend, Irwin, had written a story in that morning's paper identifying Callei as one of New England's really bad guys.

"And those idiots gave me a byline," Irwin said. Usually you wanted your name on the story – but not when the Mob would know your name – where to find you.

Few Providence hoodlums had been as well supported. Bevilacqua stayed by the door, but his presence gave the unnerving scene an aura of quasi-authority as if a low-level mobster had been free to deliver his grievance in any way he chose – with his lawyer/legislator riding shotgun.

Not to put too fine a point on it, but Callei was the personification of the sociopath. He morphed into a human approximation of violence. His job was to make sure his intentions were clear. He was succeeding with me.

Until the 1970s, when many newspapers became wary of demonstrators and installed guard desks and guards, we welcomed anyone with a story to tell. Newspapers were open to the public. Someone with a good tip or story might wander in.

Of course, someone was always unhappy with some story or other. They were, for the most part, free of threat and profane bluster. I had never seen anyone arrive anywhere with such bristling, physical menace.

Callei's anger had seemed to hit full boil as he crossed the threshold, as if a switch had been thrown in his brain. His eyes, his coiled bearing, signaled barely controlled mayhem. It would be years before the "Godfather" put conscience-free mob violence on wide display. Callei gave us a preview. We were going to stop writing "shit" about him.

Irwin didn't back away. He was as tough and uncompromising a reporter as Callei was an enforcer. Jim Wyman, the city editor, tried to be a moderating force. He stood up as if to say "Here, here." And then to explain the sanctity of this newspaper's workplace, as if this mad dog of a man would stop and listen.

A few of us were already on our feet. Would he and Irwin square off? Would we move into the arena with them?

This, I think, is where Bevilacqua spoke or gestured. You've made your point, something to that effect. Callei had seemed to be in a trance. Bevilacqua brought him back. He walked back through the soft gauntlet of steel desks, past the newsroom secretary out the doorway opening onto a bank of elevators. He shouted some further warning and left the building.

The FBI said Callei was part of the Raymond L.S. Patriarca organization. Patriarca was the crime boss of New England, it said. The city of Providence was on a first name basis with "Raymond." He was said to be a remorseless enforcer of his turf. Referring to him by his first name I think was the city's collective effort to make him seem less threatening. He was one of us. Our neighbor, the Mafia guy.

Whether designated by anyone but himself, Callei seemed to think he was in charge in the boss's absence.

Bevilacqua, on the other hand, had authority granted at the ballot box. The people elected him. They watched him move up in the legislature. He was a symbol of Italian ascendancy in Rhode Island life. It was, of course, a kind of profiling – a word we didn't have in those days. With this drama, though, Bevilacqua reinforced everything many people thought: the mob had infiltrated everything. Bevilacqua was later elected speaker of the house. And then he became Chief Judge of the Rhode Island Supreme Court.

If he had ever come into the newsroom on his own behalf, I wasn't aware of it. If he had any concern about the appearances on this day, if he worried that it might affect his coverage in the paper or standing with his peers in the legislature, it wasn't evident.

Were we watching something seismic, something that meant more than you could see? Was the mob declaring new rules to the game? You're not immune to the violence you write about. Probably, we should have been glad to see him there. Maybe he had kept it all under control.

None of us challenged Bevilacqua later.

We had survived.

Or had we?

Some years later, after I left, the newspaper went after the Mob aggressively, winning a Pulitzer Prize for its work. And then, the publisher, Michael Metcalf died in a biking accident. Or was it an accident? It looked as if someone had driven up behind him with a club or two-by four, knocking him to the street.

Mob involvement was suspected – but the newspaper, after two reporters worked the story for a year, could not show a connection.

(These stories came back to me in the summer of 2018, when a gunman shot his way into the Annapolis *Capital Gazette*, killing five staffers. Some *Capital* stories had angered him. Callei might have done something similar that day in Providence. I knew, of course, that reporters were at risk of retaliation for doing their jobs. Irwin and I could have been killed that day. Had guns been as available then as now, had mass shootings been endemic then as now – had reporters been vilified by the President of the United States – who knows if I would be writing this book?)

Assistant City Editor Monaghan insisted later there had been nothing to fear. (Memory issues arose: Had we been in the same room?) Callei had come in to complain about the way he was being identified in the newspaper.

"Why don't you guys ever print my record?" Callei had demanded, according to Jack. Stories were running without the full list of his depredations. Did he fear his bad-guy image was slipping. We would use it religiously now, he told Callei.

Then he called Bevilacqua to his desk.

"Get this thug out of here," he told the lawmaker. They left – but Callei came back that afternoon.

"Now I'm going to die," Monaghan thought.

Callei walked up to his desk. And apologized.

"Sorry about this morning," he said.

Some years later, Callei was tried for murder. As the jury was considering the case, a sheaf of newspaper articles made it into the jury room. Mistrial.

Months later, a second Callei trial convened. Now a conviction seemed certain. Unwilling to trust the work of his defense lawyers, Callei managed to leave the courthouse. But his concerns were unfounded. The jury came back with a not guilty verdict. Only in Rhode Island.

A few months later, he was found in the shallow grave reserved for victims of the Mob's inside justice. Sometimes the mob did a better job policing murderers than law enforcement.

30

Bricks, Soup and a Seat at the Table

Democratic Party Job Discussion:
Ward leader: "I got this guy over here needs a job."
Mayor: "Okay. What can he do?"
Ward leader: "Nothing."
Mayor: "Good. We won't have to train him."

Very funny unless you stood jobless in the breadlines, unless you were elderly dining on dog food, unless you were a kid with nothing for lunch. Unlettered political loyalists got jobs. The poor – and the black – had no shot up through the 1960s. Jobs and food and hard work on election day were the building blocks of loyalty but not for black people.

No one talked about poverty when I was growing up in North Carolina, not even the poor.

Fear was a conversation stopper. You didn't want to lose what little you had.

I wondered why the country didn't do something about the pain of poverty. I didn't make the connection then between vexing, in-your-face problems and inaction. At 14 or 15 I didn't see what conscience and research and reporting could accomplish.

In 1962, as I was graduating from UNC, Michael Harrington's book, *The Other America*, found surprisingly wide readership. People, many of them, cared. They were embarrassed. Affluence and hunger in America didn't compute. So Lyndon Johnson's 1964 War on Poverty was not a Texas-sized pipedream. Yes, it would be expensive, but Johnson assured us we could have "guns and butter."

And he knew JFK's administration had been working on a plan to address it.

The man was gone, but an element of competition remained between the old and the new frontiersmen. There was the political leadership rule to consider. Was there a movement, a groundswell afoot? Better get in front so you could be its leader.

Harrington wasn't preaching or shaming. He was pointing to facts many had ignored. (The shaming was inherent in the message.) His level tone, thorough reporting and "moral clarity" left no room for denial.

Johnson had seen poverty up close and personal in the hill country of Texas where he grew up. With that experience, he might have been a better anti-poverty leader than Kennedy would have been. Suddenly he had the power to act.

In his 1964 State of the Union address, he declared "unconditional war" on poverty. Failure to act, he said, was a "national disgrace. A "more just" society, he said, demanded action

An array of self-help programs got underway: Head Start, Community Schools, the Concentrated Employment and Training Act, Legal Services. The program's community action agencies were designed to be laboratories for self-improvement.

Who would oppose the self-help agenda laid out alongside Johnson's Office of Economic Opportunity cannily placed in the hands of a Kennedy relative, Sargent Shriver?

Johnson seems to have known the answer. He called Richard Daley, mayor of Chicago, the infamous big city boss whose machine had turned out a big vote for Kennedy. Johnson knew he needed Daley and, presumably, he assumed other big city mayors would follow Daley's lead.

We're with you, Daley told the president in a phone conversation, if the "wherewithal" is there. Johnson assured him there would be money, plenty of money, Washington money.

But it wasn't there in Daley's hands – or not in the way Daley assumed. In fact, the anti-poverty war theorists left Daley and other big city mayors largely out of the equation. Had he been in it, the wherewithal could have gone to the loyalists with nothing but loyalty to recommend them.

Larry McGarry, known as Mr. Democrat in Providence, became a Daley ally. Who had given poverty warriors authority to sidestep the party guys?

McGarry mocked the anti-poverty idea and the community action agency. "What do they do over there," he asked me one day when I was talking with him about something else. He threw back a shoulder, gesturing toward the new poverty program's office on Waterman Street at the foot of College Hill.

"Do they make soup? Do they make bricks?"

Mocking questions, of course, and interesting from a political boss never concerned about leaf raking. If his people held the rakes, they got the patronage jobs in which little more than loyalty was required.

Had Johnson's troops failed to understand they had to appease the bosses and boss-lets? Daniel Patrick Moynihan, a U.S. senator and scholar, assumed they made a fatal error. He wrote a book he called *Maximum Feasible Misunderstanding*.

His was a take from 40,000 feet. The poverty fighters would obviously lose versus Daley, he said. How could anyone have gone against the powerful king-maker from Chicago? Wouldn't there be hell to pay? Moynihan was right about this.

Leaving the bosses out of the "wherewithal" game was one thing. But the issue went much deeper. One of the principal ideas driving the war could be thought of as government sponsored power-to-the-people. Despite Johnson's pledge to Daley, the federal government was financing a coup against established political powers, Daley being example No 1.

Unlikely as it may have been, I wonder if the new program's designers hadn't changed things a bit without Johnson's knowledge. They feared (or just knew) the bosses would never accept a system they didn't control. Helping the poor and African Americans find a way into the political system was a critical aspect of the war – not something bosses would tolerate by definition.

And there was one other issue, a far bigger one. The anti-poverty agencies wanted to empower men and women who had never run anything. To deal with poverty, they thought, people had to be involved, engaged and committed to everything, including politics. Boss-led systems ran on loyalty and standing in line. You delivered the mail. You handed out leaflets. You made sure people voted. You took them to the polls. You did all the scut work. You had a stake in everything, the outcome of elections and often your job.

Then suddenly an outside force wanted to drive the bus.

Johnson's community action agencies bypassed Daley and McGarry. The anti-poverty program's community action agencies held elections outside party official channels. Rookie candidates of no political party campaigned and won office. The idea was to create ownership and loyalty -- just as political parties had always done – with jobs, in this case government jobs. The community action candidates and workers would have a stake in something, finally.

Chaos reigned. It felt like democracy. I covered many of the raucous community action meetings. (Like the one Dickie and Joey ran, the one where someone was murdered.)

They were tedious, interminable, exhausting and often unproductive. I loved them.

Daley cried foul. He had not signed on for a new pathway to political involvement. But he had an immediate way to push back. He had democratic allies in the U.S. Congress.

As for Larry McGarry's mocking question, no it was not soup or bricks the program sought to provide. When it was allowed to function, Johnson's war was raising voices, arming citizens bent on having a voice and reaching for justice.

When Johnson and the Rev. Martin Luther King Jr. talked to the president, he told King 70 percent of the civil right issues would be solved if blacks had the vote. The community action program, the war on poverty's coup, would give new citizens experience in running their own affairs. Fifty years later, Republicans certified John's prediction by slicing into black power. They enacted safeguards against non-existent voter fraud by making it far more difficult for voters to be registered or to vote if they were registered.

31

Henry

And there was one more regiment in the anti-poverty war, a phalanx of poverty fighters led quietly and affirmatively by community organizers. Many of them had started as priests or nuns, and in the case of Providence, by a bishop who secretly bankrolled them.

The money was coming from Catholic charities. These organizations were run under the control auspices of what one of the ex-nuns called the "sterling" Catholics of Providence. ("Sterling" meaning wealthy.) Some of them were bankers who would not have been happy to know their church's money was financing the periodic picketing of their banks.

The former priest, Henry Shelton, organized the pickets. His goal was empowerment. People gained power and status by acting. Henry's legions began to picket banks that red-lined – refusing mortgages to credit-worthy buyers in predominantly black and poor neighborhoods. Banks feared houses in such neighborhoods would lose value -- or end up in the banks' hands when the mortgage wasn't paid. The anti-redlining troops argued the banks had taken an anti-neighborhood stance. How could neighborhoods get stronger if homeowners were essentially barred?

So, as the pickets proceeded, Bishop Russell McVinney, a portly Irish cleric, unaccountably became Henry's bag man. Did he see Henry as more priestly than he? Was he embarrassed?

One morning, Sister Arlene Violet, who had ridden gumption into the state attorney general's office, saw McVinney driving himself to ex-priest Henry's South Providence community center on Prairie Avenue. This was notable. Bishops didn't drive.

This one did at least once. He got out of the dark sedan and walked into the center and directly into Henry Shelton's office. After he left, Henry summoned the staff.

"This is our budget," he said, holding up the bishop's leather satchel. Arlene estimated it held $20,000 – $150,000 or so in 2019 money. The bishop worried the money would be directed elsewhere by the "sterlings."

"McVinney had Henry's back," Violet said.

Everyone knew over time that Henry Shelton and Russell McVinney had become a team. And some of them knew that Henry and others who followed him were disciples of Saul Alinsky, the revolutionary, Back of the Yards Chicago theoretician of revolt. Alinsky's school trained generations of rabble rousers (as they were called), Henry Shelton included.

Alinsky was famous for his theories and for his definition of reconciliation. "Reconciliation," he said, "is when I get the power and you get reconciled to it."

Henry came close. He beat on members of the Rhode Island General Assembly to create utility relief for the poor in winter. A bill to that affect was named in Henry's honor. Final passage of the Henry Shelton Act occurred with enough ceremony and acclaim to make the most revolutionary organizer blush.

(I learned while researching this chapter that the nuns had gone before me into the Hartford projects. Several of them, including Arlene Violet and Carol Shelton, who married Henry when both left the church in the 1970s, lived there for a year or so.) The Sheltons had four children, leading to no cessation whatever in the former priest's life-long commitment to the poor.

From time to time, after I left the paper to work for the *Sun* in Baltimore, Henry would confront editors in Providence.

"When are you going to hire more people like Smith?" he would demand, according to Carol Young, by then one of the paper's top editors. I think Henry appreciated my work and my conviction that we were all there to afflict the comfortable. In time, he had any number of reporter allies. He wanted editorial support as well as support on the street. He knew he would always be outnumbered. If he made the newspaper feel a bit guilty, all the better.

32

Kangaroo

Newspaper bosses, I found, operated with varying degrees of authority. A lot of them seemed to have no social skills.

Then there were the martinets, men like the *Providence Journal's* managing editor, Charlie Spillman. He spent his newspaper life scowling. Did he go to bed and wake up with that scowl? Maybe he put it on in the car on his way to work? If he had another expression, I never saw it – or maybe I did, once.

He sat in his managing editor's chair in crisp, short-sleeved shirts. He ran the newspaper in the late 1960s when Route 95 was being completed. The new highway was, no doubt, big news. I wondered if it would end the joke about getting directions in New England:

Traveler: "How do I get to (fill in the blank)?"

New Englander: "Well, you can't get there from here."

Route 95 meant you could get anywhere and you could get there much more quickly.

Unless there was an accident. For Spillman, there was no such thing as a small accident. Any fender bender or tie-up had to be tracked down and reported by his newspaper. Providence drivers wanted to know why they'd been delayed the evening before.

Over time, Spillman's coverage ideas fell into a category: Charlie, it was said, "has a whim of iron."

We did what Scowling Charlie wanted. His orders reached us via Al, the city editor, who seemed even more in thrall to Charlie than the rest of us. Also in short sleeves, Al let us know what Charlie wanted. I could never tell if he ever disagreed. Why bother. He saw the whim up close and personal. It sat right behind him. Faster to just comply.

One night a reader called in to say he'd heard there was a kangaroo in the lobby of the Biltmore Hotel. Was it true? Before the internet, newspapers answered important questions about everything, including unlikely but interesting animal sightings. Or large vegetables waiting to be photographed or the inimitable night blooming cereus, a perennial:

"Night blooming cereus on line two," a copy kid or intern would announce. A sub editor would dutifully (almost always) listen and decide if anything needed to be done.

Of course something needed to be done, Charlie thought. If one person knew, the whole city might know and not the *Journal*? Not Spillman's *Journal*.

Al looked around for someone to send to the elegant downtown lodging two or three blocks from the newspaper. He didn't want to send one of his best men. Actual news might break out. Jones, the new guy, got the nod.

Ten minutes later, he was back.

"No kangaroo," he said, making no effort to hide his annoyance. Some nut job calls the desk and we jump? What kind of newspaper were we working for?

Johnson motioned for him to come forward. He didn't want anyone to hear what he would say.

"A short," Al whispered, holding his thumb and forefinger an inch or two apart. A "short" was a story of three or four inches in length.

"But there was no kangaroo," Jones said. Al might have cocked his head a bit to the right or left as if to say "Listen to me. And lower your damn voice." He made the "short" sign yet again with thumb and forefinger.

Al was doing what Spillman wanted. Here was the famous whim.

What some might see as just desserts caught up with Scowling Charley eventually.

A fairly well known state highway official died one afternoon and an obituary was ordered. Spilman knew the man. Did he ever. They were not friends. They spoke more than occasionally to discuss a poorly maintained road near Spillman's house south of the city. He drove over it – or around it –

every day. No one had come, he told the man, once again, to fill it or pave over it. Not for years, apparently.

In most situations involving the death of a public figure, Spillman would have waited to see the story in the first edition proofs. Not with this one. This one got his early, undivided attention. Dutifully, someone, the opy desk chief, brought it over and laid it on his desk.

I'd been waiting for this moment, having heard him demand to see the copy. Some of us knew of the war between our crusty editor and the highway man.

Charley read. He went carefully through the writing and editing. The deceased man's life was laid out before him. Grim-faced and focused as always, he said nothing. Apparently satisfied that his team had done its work well, he leaned forward, picked up his pen and wrote something quickly in the margin of the page. The editor who had worked on the piece, watching Charley as I was, came over to get it and take it to the composing room.

We all went back to work. An hour later, the page proofs arrived to be read for errors. By now the paper's first edition was coming off the presses. We always had one last opportunity to find and correct mistakes before the larger, later press runs. The pages were parceled out to the copy editors and to the managing editor. The idea was to find whatever misspellings and other errata had been deposited in the stories by what I came to think of as "The Gremlins," newspaper creatures that crept into every paper every day despite the multiple fact-checking redundancies built into the process.

Usually, of course, *we* were the gremlins.

As always when the time to approve a page arrived, Spillman had his pages. On "the rim," a half-rounded table, editors read stories they had not edited. The idea was to have fresh eyes on every story. Familiarity breeds blindness.

Almost immediately, Spillman leapt from his seat and ran to the fabled but almost never used, "Stop the Presses" button.

My God, I thought, what has happened?

The button got pushed when presidents were shot or when popes were chosen or when killer asteroids were upon us.

This time the skies were almost as threatening – for the button presser himself.

When Spillman had gotten to paragraph three of the highway man's obituary -- where the essence of a story usually appeared -- he found these familiar words:

"Some called him the biggest horse thief unhung in the history of Rhode Island." The observation had been written by Charley in a way that signaled his intent to have the line inserted in the story.

The whim of iron at work.

This sentence was about to land on the front steps of 150,000 subscribers.

No one had dared to say to him "Are you serious? Do you really want this in the paper?" He learned on that night how slavishly some of us adhered to his wishes. Or maybe some copy editor knew exactly what he was doing when he asked no questions.

Ten thousand or so newspapers would never leave the building. We were all interested to see another facial expression from Spillman: And there it was, sheer, white-faced terror.

33

Rockstar

When Claiborne Pell of Newport entered the 1960 race for U.S. Senate in Rhode Island, Jack Kennedy called him the most unelectable man in America. He had a point, but he missed a few things.

Tall, thin – almost gaunt – his deep, unassuming patrician voice made him seem like a grownup version of the rich kid about to be bullied. Kennedy was right about the optics. The traditional optics.

Pell brought none of the political bona fides. He'd paid no political dues – no community associations, no tours on a city council or board memberships, no House seat.

He did have two important attributes: money and a winsome way with the voters. People tended to believe it when he said he wanted to serve. These two qualifications gave him a better chance to catch lightning in a bottle.

Kennedy and many reporters who wrote about Pell were distracted by what we collectively called his otherworldly manner. We missed the tall, dark and handsome aspect of his candidacy. He was open and vulnerable. I started to get it when I saw file photographs taken during his first race. Voters – women in particular -- were drawn to him.

Out campaigning for the first time, he was awkwardly sincere, engaging, happy to meet you. Lack of polish endeared him to voters, weary of pasted-on sincerity.

He was as down to earth as an ancestor worshiper could be. He sometimes seemed posted here from an alternative universe.

He seemed not to know the difference between basketball and baseball.

And then there was his money. No one discounted that. Wealthy beyond even his New York and Newport roots, he had, political handicappers realized, an unmatchable qualification: he could have bought the state of Rhode Island all by himself. With his equally wealthy, more politically adept wife, he could pay out of petty cash.

"Guy doesn't have to steal," people said with a bet-on-that shake of the head.

His family's money and his wife's money seemed to put him out of reach of grafters. Few could have outspent or out-ranked him socially.

Kennedy may never have been so wrong about anything in his life. Pell won the first time out and five times thereafter.

As more and more Joe Nimiroskis fell in Vietnam, as the war raged on, the *Journal* raged with it. Pell became one of the war's leading (if not most effective) opponents. He met with war protesters in the square outside the Biltmore less than two blocks from the paper. He came to speak with the mostly young people gathered there to confront him. What a let-down for the protesters. He was with them.

Pell's views were shared fully then by the *Journal's* editorial page. The war was an atrocity, we'd been saying. It was prosecuted as if real and immediate U.S. interests were at stake. None of this was true, the paper wrote. Pell agreed, mostly. And there was the sense that he had arrived at this position entirely on his own. He was no tribune of anti-war sentiment, no committed pacifist. His opposition seemed to come from practicality, from what he had learned as a foreign service officer. He wanted to support President Lyndon Johnson, but decided he could not. The reach for victory in Vietnam, he thought, exceeded our grasp.

There is no suggestion that he was looking for support from the editorialists. He didn't need them. He was as strong with Rhode Islanders as any political leader in the state.

I found myself talking with him one day in his Russell Building office on Capitol Hill.

"When I think about the war," he said, reaching for his faded brown belt, "I think about my father." As portly as his son was pencil-thin, Pell senior refused to take a policy position he disagreed with and lost his re-election bid. The senator wore his father's belt as a reminder, a personal circumference of conscience.

He was a patrician and, if goofy, more effective than most of his colleagues. Stories about him were legion, oft-repeated. The first and iconic of these true stories involved shoes or to be more exact, overshoes.

Pell was campaigning one day when it began to rain. A staffer went to a nearby store, Thom McAn by name, to buy a pair for the senator.

"Where did these come from?" Pell asked. Thom McAn's, he was told.

At the end of the day, Pell peeled them off.

"Give them back to Tom and thank him very much," Pell said.

"Senator, Thom McAn's is a shoe store."

"Oh," said Pell, "I thought he was a volunteer." Volunteeah, we said, when repeating the story.

(Every year his staff sent out a Christmas season photograph of the Pell family arrayed along the Cliff Walk, a famous promontory in Newport where the Pells lived. My friend Doug Wilson, a *Journal* reporter, wrote the caption for the Senator's card one year: "Wasps On A Beach.")

I wrote a profile of him for *Change*, an education magazine, the headline for which was "Speak Softly and Carry a Small State."

On another assignment for the *Journal's* Sunday Magazine, the *Rhode Islander,* I planned a tennis outing with him one morning. He had been doing his daily dozen (push-ups, etc.) long before the nation warmed to aerobics and running. His usual routine, he said, was to put his trousers on one leg at a time, balancing for a moment on each leg. Just a little thing to maintain fitness, he professed. (Tom Hughes, the senator's press secretary, overhearing this report, whispered to me, "You do that, don't you?") He had an excellent staff. They never tried to camouflage his eccentricities. If he said something weird they tended to smile or carefully roll their eyes. Several of them had been reporters. They decided to use their man's oddness as oddly effective curiosities. Soon none of these mattered because he was changing the world.

We were to meet at his house in Georgetown and from there head toward nearby tennis courts. The senator, wearing a suit jacket carefully buttoned and sweater atop Bermuda shorts, arrived to find the courts locked. Not even slightly deterred, he climbed the fence, lowered himself inside and unlatched the gate. A *Journal* photographer was with us so we had a shot of a U.S. senator, one leg on one side of the fence one on the other.

Once after I had been assigned to the *Journal's* Washington Bureau in 1972, I was ushered into his office while he finished a phone conversation with John Hackett, a one-time vacuum cleaner of the news, then on the editorial board in Providence.

At the end of their conversation, Hackett said something like, "Well, Senator, let's just hope the Red Sox do well this weekend." The hapless Sox were in the process of tantalizing and teasing their fans with yet another run at the post season.

Pell said, "You know, John, I never watch football on TV."

A believer in the paranormal, Pell was occasionally referred to by Hill staff and some of his colleagues as Clayballs or Stillborn or something else.

He was certain he had a way around every opponent.

"Always let the other man have your way," he would say. He was, in fact, a man of insightful approaches to getting things done in life and on Capitol Hill.

Livvy or Livingston Biddle was his man on the arts and humanities; Paul Goulding a wonderful story teller, was his brilliant political man and an expert on the eccentricities of Rhode Island.

Pell outlasted Kennedy's prediction in part because he was unlike any of his peers. He accomplished politically difficult things because none of them were damaging to his voters (the opposite, more likely) and because he was strong enough at the polls to withstand usual "big spending Democrat" attacks. Also, I think, people just liked and admired him. He was real.

His main Washington office was in the Russell Office Building, but he had a smaller one deep in the Capitol itself. It had a window through which the entire expanse of the National Mall was visible straight down to the Lincoln Memorial. Hughes took me through a maze cramped corridors to the senator's splendid hideaway. What a vantage point for this eccentric man of the people.

I guess Tom thought I'd be impressed with the view. I was.

34

Big Plans, Small Minds

Newspapers, as well as men, are thus of the frame and fiber of antique Time. Old influences of which they themselves are unconscious contribute to their character. Forgotten voices speak through them.

Providence Journal writer, circa 1928,
the newspaper's 100th anniversary

Nixon and the presidency were not on my plate in 1972. Rhode Island and Claiborne Pell definitely were. Pell's tenure, always thought to be tenuous, faced its most challenging moment. His opponent would be former governor, John Chafee, experienced, affable and as much a part of the moneyed establishment as Pell.

I was moving toward a permanent assignment in the newspaper's Washington Bureau. Whoever won the race would be the primary subject of my work. All of this created difficulties. I had never covered a campaign, having spent most of my time on social welfare issues. Essentially in transit between Providence and D.C., I stayed in touch remotely reading what my colleagues were writing. I would be covering the winner as he settled into office or, in Pell's case, continued with his already remarkable work.

Of course, I knew you covered exhaustively, day by day (not minute by minute as reporters today, feeding the insatiable web). You read the issue papers, talked with campaign staff, and kept track of coverage to achieve a measure of fairness.

Contacts – campaign aides and other staff – were essential. If you were doing your job, you knew who could talk about strategy and concerns. You had some indication of who would be helpful in each camp. If you had good sources with pollsters and party officials, you had some idea of each candidate's strength and weakness. You would know what was on the collective mind of the voters. Was this a wave election or a simple a contest between an incumbent with a record and challenger with a big name?

In 1972, editors and reporters were doing all of this in Rhode Island. The paper's Washington correspondent, Ham Davis, my predecessor, *read* our paper's coverage, but had little to do with it -- until election night when, by custom, the Washington guy would big-foot into the game. No one objected. Just the way it was done. Davis would write the big winners or losers story. Slated to become his second in command, I would be watching as closely as possible. I had spent a few weeks of vacation relief, replacing him in the Washington office.

This race, it turns out, had an added layer of complexity over and above my transitional status.

The *Journal's* owners had a dog in the fight. They wanted Chafee to unseat Pell. They must have thought things were going their way. Polling showed Chafee with a substantial lead, The battle was seen by some as a struggle between two of the state's wealthiest public servant families fought out as fiercely as any political clubhouse fight.

The affable Chafee, a Republican, seemed likely finally to show that Jack Kennedy's declaration was finally coming true. Pell, he had said, was the most unelectable man in America. He had defied the pronouncement.

As the race entered its final days. *Journal* ownership seemed likely to have its man. Pell's press secretary, Tom Hughes, a former *Journal* reporter, kept tabs on the daily assignments to assure a fair shake for his man. (This sort of surveillance may have been provoked by a concern that the *Journal,* with its own candidate might abandon its usual professionalism. It did not nor would it have, absent the watchdog Hughes.)

The polls were wrong – or, at least, an incomplete measure of the campaign. Polling can't measure turnout.

Here, Pell had more than a coverage sheriff going for him. Apparently outside the purview of the *Journal's* campaign coverage team, a formidable battery of political technicians had been flown in to help with his campaign: pollsters with track records; GOTV (get out the vote) masters; targeting experts who could find every likely Democratic voter; well-connected fundraisers; candidate managers; debate coaches and others.

Pell's team commanded all this talent, not solely to save a Democratic senator, but to keep a worrisome, embarrassing Democrat out of a committee chairman's seat. Jim Eastland, a smart unreconstructed Southerner, would become chairman of an important health and welfare committee if Pell lost. Democrats were not confident in Eastland's commitment to fairness and progressive legislation, particularly since so much of the Democratic Party was black and reliant on fair treatment. Thus, did everybody send their best men to help with Pell's campaign.

The *Journal's* Pell-Chafee operation had no or little knowledge of this. They assumed the polling was accurate and gave little if any attention to the election day ground game or even to the depth of feeling that might want to keep the popular and productive Pell in office. (Never trust anyone else's poll -- or your own poll. But at least if it's yours, you know the questions, the margin of error and everything else about it. When writing, qualify liberally.)

In Washington, Davis had followed the basic rules in his Pell coverage: Go early and stay late; meet everyone that mattered in the candidate's team; spend as much time as possible with the candidate himself.

He knew early on, for example, that Pell wanted to find a way to help poor and low income students get to college. The idea of what became known as Pell grants came to the unelectable senator while he was skiing in Europe.

"Don't write the skiing part," Pell said to Davis before laying out the rudiments of his plan. Davis, who loved policy more than politics, was more than willing to make that trade.

So, when he got to Providence the day before the election and had nothing to write, he got a look at everything the campaign was doing. State of the art, he thought.

He left Pell's downtown campaign headquarters located a block or two from the newspaper.

"Pell's going to win," he said. The newsroom scoffed silently. The externals said the opposite.

Pell won – with 54% of the vote. (And so, incidentally, did Richard Nixon.) At the newspaper's request, Davis stayed to write a Sunday story explaining how the unelectable man from Newport had won yet again. His account infuriated the *Journal's* Chafee crowd. They apparently regarded his story as a shot at them. It was not. It was a good reporter with what amounted to an exclusive.

Newsroom editors had been working to secure a national column for him. The plans were ditched. He stayed at the paper several more months, then quit and moved to Vermont. He worked for the *Burlington Free Press* for a short time.

After a year or two he left that paper to run for the Vermont legislature. He won, served two years and left to become one of the most knowledgeable health care experts in the country.

35

Watergate and the Rest of Us

We were transfixed by Pell-Chafee – and by Watergate as the rest of the country. We locked into the drama. How would Woodward and Bernstein get to the Oval office? When? Where would the second-rate burglary lead? Would two relatively young reporters (like us) bring down a president?

I have wondered when they really realized the stakes. I had the sense that they were simply working to the end of the story. But when did they begin to know that Nixon was the story and that his actions would be fatal to his presidency? What turn of the cosmic kaleidoscope had taken the team to that moment?

Like Davis and I, reporters had their own stories to report and write. We were in awe of the investigative process – as much of it as we could see. The reporters in my demographic, eight or so years older than these instant stars, watched the story unfold, seeming to fade in and out of compelling. Not all of us read the *Post* every day and updates were not, as they are today, constant. So, as riveted as we may have been, we had our own work to do.

And occasionally, the story threw off a local angle, a peripheral element that mattered or was of interest to our readers. One of these side stories came to us in the form of Baruch Korff, a rabbi from Seekonk, a suburb just over the Massachusetts line.

Korff was an operator. He had acquired something of an attachment to Nixon based on the President's help with financial aid to Korff's allies in Europe during the Cold War. As the circle closed on Nixon, Korff formed a support organization. In a short period of time, he had won easy access to the White House and Nixon. (The famous Watergate tapes, among other things, suggested Nixon was prone to telling, anti-Semitic utterances. A friend in need, being a friend indeed, Korff suddenly had access to Nixon who called Korff – "my rabbi.")

I was on summer relief as Watergate gained momentum. I covered one of the rallies called by Korff, to support the president. I sat through one of these sessions at an imposing Washington hotel not far from the National Zoo on Connecticut Avenue. The evening featured fulsome encomiums. Nixon's own staff might have been embarrassed at the obsequious tone.

At the end of the evening, Korff got Nixon on the phone from San Clemente. Their brief conversation was piped into the room.

As if speaking to a king, he said, "May we take our leave from you now Mr. President."

Even Nixon may have been happy to end the fawning by then. He said thank you and broke the connection.

We had no laptops in those days only our notes. I did some minimal organization of my scribbling and dictated what I had to the city room in Providence.

I have been asked occasionally if Watergate brought me into journalism. Not at all. I was as transfixed as anyone by the drama, by the skill and daring of the *Post* reporters and editors. But every story you wrote had an element of risk and uncertainty. So there was a bit of annoyance that two lucky reporters were jousting with the President of the United States and gang of can't-shoot-strait bumblers.

Of course we knew with Watergate, routine reporting risk flew off the charts.

But no, it was not the drama or romance of that story that got me in the game. I have spoken to several of my colleagues, most of them committed newspaper people long before Watergate. We were all in with the prospect of a byline. My ex-wife Eileen says she was actually a bit miffed to see so many eager young people lining up for journalism classes at Lehigh, her alma mater. By then she had been editor for almost every paper she worked for. The importance of the work for society had been her passion long before Woodward and Bernstein.

36

Kiff

I left the *Providence Journal* in 1977. In the Washington bureau at the time, I called Jim Wyman, the city editor, to say I had a new job at the *Sun.*

"You scoundrel you," he said with a little laugh. He didn't know what to say. I didn't either. I hadn't expected much emotion from him and certainly not from me.

I choked back a sob. What's the matter with you? I said to myself. This is what you wanted, right? Moving on with your experience, finding a better paper. It would be some years before I got some understanding of that moment.

I would frequently get back to Rhode Island: a wedding, a funeral, a birthday, a vacation on Block Island. A sick friend. The state, itself, actually. Such a quirky, singular place. Would there ever be another place like it?

Cory told me years later she was furious with me. She'd found the perfect editor, the perfect teacher, the perfect role model, Don Smith. Not me – though I may have been so focused on moving up, I didn't recognize a competitive goal right in front of me.

In 2010 I went to see Kiff, John Kiffney, cancer-stricken and nearing the end of his life with as much spirit as he had lived it. He lay against his pillow like a branch torn from a tree, shrinking and losing color where it had fallen. He coughed a desperate cough. I took his hand. His grip was strong and firm, much stronger than I expected. I was always underestimating him.

He had been born with a condition that stunted the growth of his arms and legs, shortening and bending them. It had not impeded him. He walked with a driving, rhythmic upswing. Over time we forgot how impaired he was physically. Partly because we began to realize it was not an impairment in the life he chose. He was usually smiling or laughing. He loved to play golf. He played joyfully but not well. We lavished praise on his efforts. I wondered if he wasn't a little annoyed at us. Were we patronizing him? He knew we were applauding determination more than results. He never said anything. He would take what was offered and be happy about it. He had a kind of constant, electric energy and I was always impressed with his sense of humor, a completely un-macho defiance of whatever opposed him.

Now his body was moving aside, shrinking. But I thought the room was full of his aura, an even-then expanding essence of him. One last second wind seemed to flow directly from his mind. It was a force with no mooring. It was commanding and soothing. The cancer had flattened out some of the hurried way he spoke. He was less buffeted by his own nervous enthusiasm.

It had been a few years since we were reporters together. He was part of an earlier time that came unexpectedly flooding back. Others had been closer to him than I, but I liked him and he seemed a link to a past I suddenly missed terribly. It was a revelation to me. A dying man was reviving some years of my life, years I had left behind physically but not emotionally. I had internalized the advice I had gotten about gaining newspaper experience and selling it. That was the way you got ahead in what we called "the business." That was how you ended up working on a succession of papers, one better than the one before. That was the goal – more than the goal of finding a life with good friends and a way of living. Standing by Kiffney's bed, I thought myself guilty of literally selling a part of myself, a part I had valued, a part I had, until that moment, almost forgotten. The realization was the gift. Leaving people was not a mistake he would have made. On the day I visited, his parents were in town from upstate New York. As frail and weak as he was, he took over the introductions. He was going on a spurt, yet another second wind. He was dismissing yet another affliction as he always had. He was rejoicing in the work we had done – done together.

He described for his mother and father the jobs we all had when we worked at the *Journal*. He did all of this with relish and detail, affirming our joint enterprise. It was a declaration of pride. Shared pride. The sharing was what seemed to matter most to him and, suddenly, to me. It seemed a comfort to him. It was to me.

While I was there, Kiffney and his wife, Sheila, opened a package of books someone had sent. He set them on a side table as if for the moment. Of course, there would be no time for them. They were like a wall between the moment and future he would not know. And that, too, was fine.

If the recognition troubled him there was no indication. I didn't acknowledge his dying directly but he did. He said he was not going to get better. "We're handling this with a little class – to the surprise of a lot of people," he said.

No one is surprised, I should have said. People had seen his courage and his generosity. He put his shortened arms around new reporters, knowing the lost feeling that came with a new job. People remembered.

That's what I was thinking. I think he did know how people felt about him. But I wondered if he knew well enough when he was not so sick. I suppose we are all struggling to show who we are and how we feel about each other and never sure of how or if we succeed or fail.

He told us that day about this house where he would die. After he and Sheila bought it, he thought he might walk to work maybe 5 miles away to the newspaper office in downtown Providence. It would be a challenge and a tonic. He could go through Roger Williams Park. I wondered how he would have looked, throwing his body forward with that herky jerky rhythm. And then the cancer came.

He settled for his porch. Friends carried him down to a couch there. One evening, sitting with his wife, he talked about his funeral. There would be a lot of detail and expense so he decided on cremation. He declared it suddenly and the conversation turned to a memorial service.

About a week after my visit, he died. I took the train back to Providence and then a bus to Roger Williams Park where the service would be held. I wanted to take a little of the walk he'd been denied. The park is a fine progression of quiet spaces laced together by dark ponds, greenhouses, a pony ride, a smelly zoo and a carousel. On this day, a ceremonial, solitary red flower bloomed in the middle of one pond. A woman and a small child cruised around in one of the paddle boats. Adults and children danced as a group called the Melody Play Boys performed.

The service was held in front of a small white band shell. There was chamber music. A white poster made by friends and decorated with ribbons and colored markers read, "Good bye, Kiff. We love you."

Friends spoke. Marty Funk, a drinking buddy, recalled asking him if he had thought about dying and if he was afraid. Yes, he said he had thought about it and that he was not afraid.

"I think I've got it in perspective," he said. If anyone was unafraid of dying, if anyone had his own death in perspective, Marty said, it was Kiffney.

It wasn't necessary to be unafraid or to have your death in perspective, but I thought Marty was probably right. And most of all I was grateful to him for having asked. It gave us all another example of a life well-lived.

After the service, we went back to John and Sheila's house. On a table in the front hallway, there was a photograph of him in a golf hat. At first, I thought he wore it to cover the chemo-driven baldness. But he never really cared how he looked. He was always a bit disheveled, his hair disarrayed by constant nervous twirling. At the same time, there had always been a rakishness about him. The photograph with the golf hat was a last word – a "kicker" we called it in the business – a wink at the fates.

Part III:

The *Sunpapers*

1977-2006

The Newspaper and the City

Vignette: A brief, evocative description, a literary sketch.

My newspaper vocabulary did not include the word. I'd thought of "vignette" in the usual literary sense, as a telling, even teasing, introduction to some longer piece of writing.

But the newspapers (via Mencken), it is said) re-purposed the word as a kind of mission statement. The *Sun's* reaches out every day on page one with a line drawing that tells the newspaper's story which parallels the city's. It must surely be the classiest of the genre.

The basic, unique aspects of Baltimore find their way into the drama. The eye falls quickly on the iconic Baltimore clipper. The bald eagle, wings spread above a flag motif, protects democracy. The Greek goddess, Themis, holding a scale and a broad sword – justice and enforcement. Grains of wheat suggest prosperity. A church steeple rises in the background. Everything is here but the city's well-scrubbed marble steps.

The *Sun's* muscular beginning in 1828 paralleled the city's. (Muscular? The printer-publisher's decision to serve the citizenry as a whole, not just its businesses, drew instant subscribers. Many of them. A half-dozen competitors were gone in a year.)

The newspaper lampooned or praised everything city government did. Its editors took a stance on issues daily. The vignette, though altered occasionally, renewed the Sun's role in democracy every day. No disagreement, however fierce, threatened that. The *Sun* and Baltimore were one.

Could either survive without the other?

A New Neighborhood

President Kennedy, we were told, read the *Sun* every morning. The paper had eight foreign bureaus then. It had a large Washington presence. It was always mentioned in the list of America's best newspapers. Why wouldn't I want to be with that paper?

I was moving in the prescribed upward direction. And yet I was leaving 14 years of my life – friendships, colleagues and newspaper times. There would be a cost to leaving. (My career coach left that part out.)

New challenges loomed. I knew I was up to them. I just had to get settled.

Single again by then, I found a small, third floor apartment in Bolton Hill, one of the city's most distinctive neighborhoods. Distinctive in several ways. It might be one of the nation's most elegant, gated urban communities.

The barriers were invisible, untended unless you consider the power of law to shape a citizenry for a century or more. My new neighborhood was almost 100 percent white. Black people stayed away by pattern and practice, not by law.

That was not always so. In the early 1900s, an ordinance tried to stabilize Baltimore's racial composition. Neither black nor white families could move into a neighborhood if their presence would tip the racial balance. If the neighborhood was black in 1910, no whites could move there – as if that were likely. Blacks were to stay in their place – a thinly veiled Jim Crow contrivance.

The Baltimore law, copied by a number of other states, was found unconstitutional a decade later but dividing lines were drawn in the city's consciousness. The lines held. They held when I lived in Bolton Hill briefly in the 1980s. They hold today for the most part, reinforced by economic standing and generations-long habit. The handsome, three-story walk-ups are accented at the boundaries by churches, synagogues and intractable, worsening poverty. Save for an occasional break-in, Bolton Hill remains a relatively safe and largely white enclave.

I had been hired to write about neighborhoods.

Bolton Hill would have been one of my first subjects – if I ever did the neighborhood job. I never did.

Before I could buy a city map, my new bosses sent me to Annapolis to cover the Maryland General Assembly then convening for its 1978 session. One of the regulars had hurt his back. Next man up.

I had come to Baltimore from Washington where, someone assumed, I had covered the Congress and more specifically that I knew something about a legislature, how bills were passed, etc. I knew what your average college freshman knows. Which, in practice, meant I knew next to nothing. Rhode Island's two senators and two representatives seldom did anything that required knowledge of the unseen bill-passing process

With my new assignment in hand, I drove to Annapolis immediately. I parked and walked past St. Anne's Church to the State House. I walked past the governor's residence called Government House, took the half-block wide State House steps two at a time, leaving the gleaming brass handrail untouched. I was psyched.

I would learn more about the history I was about to be a part of.

I stood on the checkered black and white marble floor between the House and Senate chambers. Just ahead on the central stairway I saw a painting of George Washington resigning his commission in the Continental Army. Annapolis, then the U.S. capital, was the last stop on his East Coast victory tour. Washington spoke to tearful state senators and delegates on December 23, 1783.

Everything the man did made history of course. And here he was delivering one of the most important resignations in the world's history of resignations.

The Father of the Nation, still afloat on the surge of revolutionary ardor, had nearly died along with his men to make the moment possible. For him and for the nation, it was a matter of life and death. The general and his army had fought to preserve an idea: self-government. He might have been made king. The people revered him. He demurred. He had determined to walk away from such an investiture.

> ...I resign with satisfaction the appointment I accepted with diffidence; a diffidence in my abilities to accomplish so arduous a task; which however was superseded by a confidence in the rectitude of our cause, the support of the supreme power of the Union, and the patronage of Heaven.

He had to steady himself as he read his hand-written speech. He spoke with an eye to the future. His text, which has survived, has him bidding an "affectionate farewell" with the word "final" crossed out. Similarly, instead of "ultimate taking leave of all employments of public life" he had crossed out "ultimate."

He knew precisely what he has doing – and not doing. He wanted to reinforce the concept of civilian rule. If the people or their representatives summoned him, he would be available. Here was the essence of the man and moment.

In Annapolis for his official departure, he was toasted formally 13 times, once for each colony. Every drop of spirits, every seafood delicacy arrived for the party. Since the General might arrive after dark, every ounce of candle wax had been collected from taverns and households so as to illuminate every window in the building, its architectural style a cross between the governmental and the nautical. The towering dome had a ship of state aspect, I thought.

After the celebratory food and drink, after dancing with his hostesses, Washington headed to Mt. Vernon.

He had taken his leave of the military in a building where the laws of Maryland would be made by elected senators and delegates. The building serves as a museum commemorating the wisdom and commitment of Washington – and the effort of his successors – just short of 200 years on – to be worthy of the people's trust. His studied reluctance merged easily with the foresight of the founders.

The entire scene conveyed majesty. Something remarkable had happened here. Men, later women, were managing the people's business.

I would have the privilege of writing about the successors to Washington's 1783 audiences.

I had seen myself as part of this picture. (So modest.)

Of necessity, I cared more about the chambers a few doors west – the House of Delegates and State Senate. I would report what happened in these august precincts with as much energy as I could find – because I was competing with other reporters and because I had imbued myself with the responsibility. The voters, the citizens could not be here. They paid me (by buying the *Sun*) for the privilege.

I will admit thinking one more thing. The marble staircases, capacious, massive and yet beautiful, conveyed me – and governors – to important moments in the House and Senate chambers. I seldom if ever alluded to the history: Washington and the gift of his resignation, his character. Farther on in the State House lobby was the old Senate chamber, the room where Washington spoke.

I did not think on this day of the irony: Washington, the freedom loving slave owner. There were but 13 colonies, to be sure, and the pomp would come later. It had taken that 200 years, actually, to see a representation of that history: statues of the former slave and statesman, Frederick Douglass, and of Harriett Tubman, chief engineer of the underground railroad. Both were added in 2015.

Nor did I have much of an opportunity to remind people of what a wonder of democracy had occurred there. My job was to record "what happened yesterday."

Pinnacle

Once again, I was jumping on a moving train.

The governor of Maryland then was Blair Lee 3rd. He was actually just the acting governor. He took over when Gov. Marvin Mandel was being convicted of political corruption. His downfall ended after 22 months of folding sheets and pillow slips at a Florida prison. Mandel escaped further shame when questions were raised about the intent of Congress. Had it actually meant to target office holders whose crimes amounted to the denial of good government? While that question was being answered, Mandel was freed. Months later, Congress said that was indeed its intention.

I imagined Blair Lee pausing, as he walked to meetings, in the awe-inspiring building, to consider his own place in Maryland and national history. Walking down the imposing marble-bordered steps from his second-floor office, he could think of himself as a link in the chain of U.S. history. And, in fact, he was a link. His Virginia forebear, Richard Henry Lee, a Founding Father, had helped to shape the nation. And there he was, Francis Preston Blair Lee 3rd, passionate student of history from student days at Princeton, serving his state at a moment of great trial, a moment that called him to serve with strength and purpose.

Maryland lived then in a pit of shame. Mandel's predecessor, Spiro Agnew, had been forced to resign the vice presidency under a cloud of self-dealing. He had taken payoffs for favors granted when he was Baltimore County executive. And now a Lee would be tasked by the fates to see his constituents through a dark period – and to separate himself from the wrongdoers.

I saw Lee occasionally leaving Government House on his way to lunch. He would walk from the mansion through the gates with one of his aides, Shep Abell (a descendent of the *Sun's* founder, A.S. Abell) and always a state trooper body guard. They strolled slowly around the brick walk encircling the capitol building on State Circle and ducked down one of the stone alleyways to Main Street and his favorite lunch spot, a French restaurant called the Auberge.

He was often smoking as he walked. He smiled broadly to be sure, but there was no Rooseveltian cigarette holder panache. He did not seem burdened with the task before him – and, to be sure, he had had no part in the self-dealing that disfigured government service. Corruption would not cloud the delectable prospect of lunch – Chesapeake Bay striped bass, perhaps, or the incomparable blue crab.

And yet the circumstances might well have preoccupied him. His patron, the man who had made him lieutenant governor, loomed as a shadow over his future.

Lee ran 1978 to succeed him. To many he had seemed an almost certain winner – with the likely endorsement of the *Sun* and the *Washington Post*. Indeed, all the Maryland newspapers. I had not been in Maryland for the Mandel years, but I would be there for the transition.

Lee was a clean break. Inside the political cocoon, he was regarded as oddly inexperienced. He'd been a state senator and secretary of state afterall. If this looked like a lack of seasoning, that was regarded as a good thing. He hadn't been around long enough to lose his idealism. In truth, he needed more experience in the scrum of politics – and he needed to want winning more than he seemed to. His father had been a power in state politics, so some of what he had accomplished he owed to this powerhouse leader once thought to be a governor in waiting. At one point in the elder Lee's life he had been virtually a co-governor.

When the old man heard his son was being offered the role of Mandel's second in command, he reportedly said, "Take it. Take it. Take it." Take it he had.

He became a central player in one of the moments that confer power on a newspaper, the *Sun*, in this case. A constant in the life of Maryland for a century and a half, the newspaper's editors stepped up to join the voters in a search for new leadership.

Lee might have been that leader.

But he would have to convince the newspaper and the citizens that he offered a sufficiently clear separation from the Mandel organization.

I watched it all from a remove, not having been in Maryland or at the *Sun* long enough to have a role in the coverage. Once again, I was learning on the run – the landscape and the players.

The need for change was the driver. The players were Lee and four other candidates: Harry R. Hughes, a former state senator who resigned as Mandel's Transportation Secretary citing pressure to award a contract to Mandel insiders; Ted Venetoulis, Baltimore County executive; Harry McGuirk, a Baltimore ward leader and shrewd operator known as "Soft Shoes;" and Wally Orlinsky, president of the Baltimore City Council. None of them seemed to find traction. Lee led by large margins from the start.

Hughes, in particular, ran poorly, barely escaping the single digits in polling. But he performed well in a late televised debate. For his part in this faceoff, Lee offered little more than a plaintiff protest to those who wanted a plague on all the houses: All politicians are not crooks, he said weakly. Hughes was judged the more statesmanlike, holding himself out of the unseemly fray. But so what? He was out of the running. (One of his opponents, McGuirk, called him "a ball lost in high grass").

But the assumption that Lee would enjoy newspaper support did not hold – was, in fact, dramatically, reversed. The *Evening Sun's* assertive Brad Jacobs prevailed by moving into a vacuum. He wanted Hughes. And, in a sense, he wanted the newspaper to fall on its inkwell. Even if Hughes didn't win – as seemed very likely at the time – The *Sun* would be on the side of the angels. For many in the editorial department, this argument had a moral edge. A sharp break from and disavowal of Mandel was imperative. The polls showed Lee having satisfied this demand.

Not for Jacobs. He saw himself as a man in a position to do something important, to galvanize a newspaper to be the kind of force a newspaper should be. He had just the right mix of authority and outrage.

Joe Sterne, the morning Sun's chief editorial writer, told me that story.

"We went through a few days of discussion and then came a unanimous conclusion: Win or lose, Harry Hughes was the best. We went to [the publisher's] house to say we wanted to endorse the guy regardless of his chances." Publishers can veto such choices, but chose not to in this case.

"We then planned an endorsement for the *Sunday Sun*. It ran in the regular place in the papers. We made a big deal of it. The whole editorial column top to bottom of the page. John O'Donnell (then an editorial writer) worked on it.

"Then Brad came in the next Monday with a front-page editorial. It was a blockbuster event. A lot of the voters felt the way we did. It seemed like a hurricane swept through the state."

It's almost an article of faith among political reporters that many voters don't tune into elections, whatever their importance, until the last two weeks. The endorsements came, then, just as voters were taking a look at the contest.

Part two of the drama came with the publication of various polls. The first of these showed Hughes falling farther behind. Then he started to move up. This candidate who had truly been lost in tall grass was gaining traction. The *Sun's* polltakers would say later that Hughes was actually showing greater movement than they were comfortable reporting. He had been so firmly cemented into the public consciousness as a lost cause that they were not willing to suddenly give him a chance. They were afraid of risking their professional standing. For the insiders, immersed in the campaign for months, the dynamics of the race seemed to be changing at high speed.

Voters wanted a role in the selection of new leadership – but, the theory went, they didn't want to "waste" their vote on someone with no chance.

"I like you Harry, but you've got no shot," he heard over and over.

Now, though, he had the *Sun's* endorsement. And the polls were moving in his direction.

If he had been lost, as McGuirk slyly asserted, suddenly he was findable. In his editorial for the *Evening Sun*, Jacobs said, "A vote for the right man is never wrong." Political observers would quote that line over and over in subsequent years.

In his political memoir, Hughes wrote, "Even today it is hard for me to find the words to describe my personal feelings about the endorsement, not to mention what it meant to my campaign. Here was the most influential newspaper in the state swinging its power through an unprecedented front page endorsement to a candidate who had never risen higher than 8 percent in any of the pre-primary polls. It was stunning."

"A clean slate" may always have been the voters' hope. If so, the *Sun's* endorsement, ratifying the common view, couldn't have been better timed. The moment surely ranks as one of the most dramatic illustrations of a newspaper's importance in a community. Its opinion writers had done what its most seasoned thinkers wanted it to do – after discussion, lobbying and weighing so many elements in the balance. It was classic, in keeping with pure democratic thinking.

Overall, the newspaper stood on the side of change even when polls gave change little hope. The newspaper and a majority of the voters were of one mind even if it took near magic to illustrate that one-ness. Editorial writer and voter found a way to the same conclusion. The newspaper as a forceful player in a community's decision-making; its considered judgment on the way forward; its role as a player in the festival of democracy – all these things ended with a win for Maryland.

Years later, the moment would be seen as the high point of *Sun* power.

40

Nothing Could Be Done with Such Men

A high point, to be sure, but a point fully in keeping with the original owners' credo.

Good newspapers had rules against any sort of relationship with public figures or lobbyists. If reporters dined or drank with politicians they were to pick up the check.

At the *Baltimore Sun*, I learned years later, the Democratic Party 1890-era bosses openly courted the newspaper's editorial staff. The paper opposed them at every turn.

Okay, what did the paper want? One party leader asked finally. Democrats in power nationally offered one of the founder Abell's sons the ambassadorship to the Court of St. James. Young Abell laughed. (Here another measure of the *Sun's* stature.)

With this fabulous offer rejected, the bosses lamented in effect: "Nothing could be done with such men."

The paper took obsessive care in keeping its distance from bankers, car dealers, realtors and developers. Publisher William Schmick famously spent pre-dinner time finding a place away from any of the commercial big noises, determined not to sit with any of them at the head table, lest someone think he had a preference for one bank over another.

As a matter of practice, the newspaper chose not to mention the name of a store or other business hit by a fire or robbery lest that be seen as favoring the said business. Should Hutzler's department store in Baltimore be so afflicted, the newspaper would identify the fire's location as 101 Saratoga Street.

In the 1980s when the newspaper began to cover consumer affairs, one of the car dealers came to complain about a story exploring car salesman shenanigans. If that sort of coverage did not end, he told the publisher, he was pulling his rather substantial ads.

"Be my guest," Schmick said.

The man turned and left. After a month or so, he returned suggesting his punishment of the *Sun* had run its course. He was ready to re-start his advertising.

"Well, thank you," Schmick said. "But we really don't have any space right now. We'll call you if that situation changes." The *Sun* would decide who could advertise in its pages. It was not beholden to any car or furniture or banking force. The protesting dealer, hurting more and more in the ad blackout, kept calling and was finally invited back.

41

Ettlin

Back in the day, no long-time Baltimore business would have tried to muscle the *Sun's* publisher into anything untoward. They had seen or heard of a Schmick or a Schmick predecessor pacing in front of the dias looking for an unbiased seat.

That was the leadership seeing the tone, defining the culture and sticking to it to the point of creating a folklore. The commentary held that *Sun* owners made their money in other enterprises and ran the paper as a public service.

They handled the business ethics. They wanted the paper to run on its standards and rules. Occasionally he was known to walk through the city room and ask (later) "Why isn't everyone typing?" He had no sense of the ebb and the flow, the deadlines, the down times. For us, his ignorance was our bliss.

We ran efficiently because of men like David Ettlin, a less than classic *Sun* man (no Ivy League background). He was the guy in the iconic poster that shows some hack – hat on in the newsroom, on the phone saying, "Hello, Sweetheart. Get me re-write." David Ettlin was re-write.

He knew the city supremely well, too, and made himself available to new reporters who didn't know that Holluntayon was actually Baltimoerese for Highlandtown. He became expert in everything he did. So, despite the grating laugh, Ettlin became one of the most valuable men at the newspaper.

He took me on a tour of the composing room, a floor beneath the newsroom. He knew the insanely jealous denizens of this critical space. He knew the relationships between the (mostly deaf) linotype operators and the makeup boss; he knew that used type was dumped in a "hellbox" and "the stone" where stories were made to fit the available space. Most of all, he knew not to touch a page at any time without permission of the proud craftsmen who reigned there unchallenged.

Years after he came to the paper, Ettlin would have been on more people's list of the paper's most valuable players.

He had a kind of goofy laugh that burst into a conversation to emphasize a point that meant more to him than to whomever he was speaking. I had to forget the laugh to hear what he had to say which was often insightful. He was both clear and detailed in his recall. He had come to the paper a decade earlier to babysit the wires.

"You'll leave in six months," said the editor who hired him in 1967. "You've got some education and you'll get bored and leave."

"No, I won't," said Ettlin. "I'm going to do a great job and you'll promote me." And so it was.

He made a bit of history in the process. Over time, his efficiency attracted adherents in the city room. Charles Whiteford, a political reporter and editor, became his rabbi – someone who spoke well of him and tipped him if there was a job opening. Openings were posted, but if you had advance notice... Ettlin succeeded, as it turned out, the newspaper's first black reporter – even as he himself was almost a first.

He had experience and no (completed) college degree. He was not an Ivy Leaguer, the newspaper's seeming historic preference. That tradition was changing, though, and Ettlin, with all his energy and smarts, was the beneficiary.

He was not hired to be a reporter. But he knew it would happen. He was promoted October 1968. He did well in all the jobs assigned to him: police, obituaries, features, re-write and editor. He became an expert in everything he did. He was like the famous *New York Times* reporter who, is was said, came into every story knowing nothing, and left knowing everything. So, despite the grating laugh, Ettlin became one of the most valuable men at the newspaper. He could pick up a story from the Middle East, a story dictated without benefit of a written story, and make it sing.

He was eventually made an assistant bureau chief in the Baltimore County bureau. He made the trip out there with all the deadline consciousness of any straw boss on Calvert Street, the newspaper's headquarters. Soon after arriving, one of the reporters motioned him over to her desk. She was pregnant and over-due.

"I think my water broke," she said.

Ettlin says he paused momentarily before offering the proper editor's response.

"Why don't you knock out that story and get out of here."

Story first, baby later.

42

Clown Car

William Donald Schaefer was about to become the most well-known mayor in the country. No one would know him as well as I did over the next decade.

He was leaving City Hall one morning as I arrived.

"Mayor Schaefer?"

He kept walking.

"My name is Fraser Smith. I'm going to be the *Sun's* City Hall reporter. I was hoping I might stop by for a chat."

As soon as I said *Sun*, Schaefer screwed up his face as if something foul had landed in his mouth, or as if preparing to spit. The reaction was so clearly an act it was almost funny.

I stuck out my hand. Schaefer ignored it. Kept walking.

I had heard of him while I was working for the *Providence Journal* in its Washington bureau. A bit of a galoot, people said, but a rebuilder in a city that needed rebuilding – in almost every way including most importantly, it was said, spiritually.

I had never covered a mayor or governor. But there were always political leaders who enjoyed baiting and stiffing the press. The tactic was almost to be expected, though probably it would not appear at "hello." Schaefer's view, I thought: if you were a reporter you had nothing to recommend you.

I quickly learned, Baltimore City Hall was a character magnet. There was a long-time employee of no known title or job who may actually have lived there. He was reportedly seen once padding down a hall in shower clogs.

Another man of mysterious importance manned a desk in the center of the building's atrium lobby. His seat was directly below the dome. What, actually, did he do?

Schaefer's predecessor, Tommy D'Alesandro Jr. (aka Young Tommy) told reporters: "He's there to watch the dome. If it starts to fall he's to call me immediately." The man worked nights as well, playing trombone in one of the "gentleman's" clubs on Baltimore's famous girlie district known as The Block.

"The Baltimore City Council," I heard early on, "is the best argument yet for the divine right of kings." I saw a group of dispirited men and women who had succumbed to their lack of power. Their chamber had become a forum. The speakers were out to make names for themselves. They had no hope of getting much done.

Schaefer and his backers owned at least 10 of the council members. The name of the game was said to be the majority: 10 votes, 10 of the 21 – not the merits of any given issue.

An exception was Council President Walter Orlinsky, a brilliant man who chose to butt heads with Schaefer on almost every issue. He seldom if ever won. He had become, by the time I got there, proof of Schaefer's control. Win or lose, he was a player. Maybe that was enough for him. Or maybe perpetually losing led him to take a payoff.

"Think of me for ten (thousand)," he told an undercover cop wearing a wire. He served time and came back to run a tree-planting program for the state. Someone in government felt sorry for him. May actually have been Schaefer, who had connections.

At my first Monday evening council meeting, I met Eddie Fenton, a radio reporter who operated as if he had a vote. He said hello to me with about the same level of courtesy the mayor had shown I thought of Eddie as "The Quasimodo of the Hall": fat, sloppy, stooped over with a few missing teeth and no respect for the council. All of them, including Fenton, thought of this governing body with something less than disdain.

Fenton would start to bellow if anyone seemed likely to stay on his or her feet for more than two minutes.

Monday Night Football had been introduced.

"The game. The game. Starts in 15 minutes," Fenton warned from the corner of the high ceilinged, varnish-brightened room. If the speaker showed no sign of taking a seat, Fenton's volume would rise.

"Wrap it up," he ordered, with just an edge of "or else" in his voice.

I wondered years later if Schaefer hadn't found a good use for all this depressing spectacle. Citizens stopped listening or reading about the high jinx. The power imbalance between council and mayor precluded any useful exchange of views. Everyone tuned out. My advantage? I was new. I had to ask questions my competition thought had been answered satisfactorily.

So, when a minor-seeming question arose about spending by Baltimore's city-owned museum, board members and reporters skipped onto the next agenda item.

But why did Baltimore have a museum? What sort of collection was there in that elegant old building? My question to myself went unanswered. I really didn't have time to inquire further. Not then. No drama here, I thought. No big money involved. Just something to check out for the record. You never knew when something mattered more than you thought. If a question occurs to you, ask it especially if you think you might be embarrassed..

I called the museum and I was told to get lost, basically. Wait a minute, I just need a quick explanation of this expenditure. The question was raised by the city auditor.

The museum was not really a city facility, I was told. Its managers had no obligation to answer my questions.

"You're a city facility," I said. "What goes on over there is public business, especially when money is the issue."

"No, we're not city," I was told again.

"What are you then?" I asked.

"A quasi-governmental agency," I was told. I was familiar with the term but only vaguely. The private part was refusing to respond to my quite innocent inquiry.

Red Flag!

What followed over the next five months was an investigation of what turned out to be a large parallel government – established over time secretly for the usual suspect reasons in such matters: efficiency and speed. Officials looking for ways around regulations or the law fell back again on speed and efficiency. The mayor's soon to be famous "Do It Now" motto was harder to obey, if you had regulations to follow.

In this case, the quasi-government structure allowed Schaefer and his green-eyeshade wizards to raise substantial sums of money in shadowy, secretive ways. They turned the city into a bank with $100 million to be used for projects the real banks found too risky.

Much if not all of it was hidden from reporters and voters. Hidden in plain sight. The bank's projects were approved in public by the Trustees of Loans and Guarantee. Somehow that entity slid into the government lexicon without real definition. After a few of its activities went through the Board of Estimates agenda, it became part of the wallpaper, part of the public action of the board – though no one really saw the scope or understood the mechanism.

Others may have concluded there was nothing to discover or report. I was new. I had to ask the questions.

The reporting/newspaper system had fallen into place inadvertently over decades. Reporters came and went. New eyes had 20-20 vision. Older ones, dulled and blinded. Questions had been asked and answered over and over. On to the next thing. If you were new, you had to overcome the embarrassment of not knowing what everyone else thought he or she knew. Sometimes the scrum of reporters bought answers without fully absorbing them. There were other issues, other questions, other explainers. If the reader was lucky, someone new took the time to dig, which often involved saying "I don't understand. I don't get it. Please tell me again. Yes, I know you just told me, but I'm not there yet...' (If such matters were so easily hidden in plain sight, what will happen when there are no or only now-and-then reporters in City Hall?)

The answers in this case led to my eight-day "Shadow Government" series with 22 articles. I found no criminal activity. What I found was a pop-up system vulnerable to manipulation and misuse – and one the voters had no knowledge of. These kinds of stories prevent scandal. They are the everyday findings of nosy, inquisitive, new reporters with beats.

The basics remain: come early, stay late, ask questions. Who else was going to do this? The council president had no power; the council was a joke; the Board of Estimates had five members, three of whom were appointed by the mayor whose projects were going forward on the strength of Shadow-generated money.

As a result of my investigation, the city treasurer began to act on his own concerns about the Shadow. Too many projects were underway, he said. His office could not keep up with them. He was concerned about a reporter's questions. A professional with pride, he stepped away from Schaefer to raise his own red flag. The newspaper, even before my report, was stimulating application of checks and balances, finding risky practices mayors wished to hide.

Soon after the series ran, the *Sun* got a new publisher, Reg Murphy, late of the *Atlanta Constitution* and the *San Francisco Examiner*. Murphy was no fan of the series, to put it mildly. Follow up stories done after I had been assigned to the Washington Bureau were routinely greeted by Murphy with disdain.

"Still beating that horse?" he said to Steve Luxenberg who had edited the project with Gil Watson, the newspaper's second ranking editor.

"Yes," we are, said Luxenberg. "It's not a dead horse unless you think $100 million in secret city hall funds is a dead horse."

Ultimately, I concluded, important stories were brushed aside because they dealt with problems before they were game for investigative reporters. Major prize hunters found big stories that got bigger in the dark. How much more money would have been spent outside the voters' approval in Baltimore without the *Sun* doing its job? And who will be the sheriff in the brave new world of news deserts? Will the ghosts be up to the job?

Notwithstanding our frequent confrontations, I thought Schaefer's career had been uniquely productive, beyond colorful – a model of public service. I proposed a book. I heard nothing. Months passed.

Then I heard he was unhappy at a law firm where he had little if anything to do. One of his brilliant aides, a state government cabinet secretary, Marion Pines, arranged a conversation over lunch at the Johns Hopkins University President's Club.

We had barely gotten seated when she said, "This man wants to write a book about you. Will you cooperate?"

"Oh sure," he said, as if the idea was brand new to him. A year or so later, Hopkins Press published *William Donald Schaefer: A Political Biography*.

C. Fraser Smith was a reporter for the *Jersey Journal* and the *Providence Journal* before his decades-long affiliation with the *Baltimore Sun* as a reporter and then Sunday op-ed columnist. In addition, while in Baltimore, he became a commentator for WYPR, the Baltimore affiliate of National Public Radio, as well as a weekly columnist for *The Daily Record,* a regional business newspaper based in Baltimore.

The Daily Miracle, A Memoir of Newspapering is his fourth book. His others include *William Donald Schaefer, A Political Biography; Here Lies Jim Crow: Civil Rights in Maryland; and Lenny, Lefty and the Chancellor: The Len Bias Tragedy and the Search for Reform in Big Time College Basketball.*

43

The "Hard" Vote

In my first years in Annapolis, "covered loads" and "eye drops" were the perennial bills. Others enjoyed long, remunerative lives, generating handsome fees, sending lobbyists' kids to college. Truckers and trucking companies paid handsomely to fend off regulations – whether or not the state could require loads to be covered. More cars encountered broken windshields and drivers exerted more and more pressure to keep flying objects off the increasingly crowded roadways.

The legislator, banker and wit, Bobby Neall, claimed to know that as he left Maryland after resigning his commission, Washington had shouted over his shoulder, "Don't cover the loads."

And so rocks flew unrestrained for decades. Had there been a lobbyist with the auto glass lobbying gig, he, too, might have quoted the father of our country.

There were, of course, matters of immediate concern. The assembly is, if nothing else, a forum for deciding winners and losers in the world of commerce. Who could protect or enable a client with regulations that helped or harmed an opponent? Handsome incomes came to those lobbyists who made sure only their clients – ophthalmologists or optometrists, for example – would have that license. Bruce Bereano won the eyedrop bill for the ophthalmologists year after year. His battle achieved hardy perennial status.

But,what really got the attention of legislators was the state's Triple A Bond rating. Since Maryland was so overwhelmingly big D Democratic, many Marylanders thought its legislature was full of big spenders. Not so.

Historically, the new voter with any interest in politics registered Democratic. Only way to be in the game as a candidate or voter.

The result? Many Democrats might be more Republican in their thinking, resulting in more conservative policy positions for the state.

The deeply Democratic image derived also from our proximity to Washington where completing a budget of any kind was always challenging,

Maryland never failed to get its spending in order. And its budget has to be balanced by law. This is one of the reasons Wall Street's scolds gave the state high marks for government efficiency, including the low interest credit rating. Nothing was more important than keeping it. Nothing created as much bi-partisanship. The higher the rating, the lower cost of borrowing. The value of the rating was there in the numbers and the money saving but it also conveyed a sense that Maryland was well-run, efficiently managed, disciplined, and truly careful with the voters' money.

Thus, did I witness one of the most ferocious legislative battles ever in Annapolis.

In a fit of daring excess, the Democrats, in 1983, buckled under to pressure from state employees and teachers to grant them almost total immunity from inflation-driven erosion of their pensions. The resulting un-capped cost of living adjustment meant pensions would rise with the cost of living: 5-20 percent – whatever.

Ruinous, Wall Street warned. Repeal it or say goodbye to the AAA.

State officials said they had no choice but to comply. If anything mattered more than covered loads it was maintaining the AAA. The letters were engraved on the culture of the place. If it was found nowhere else, bi-partisanship was there for the high bond rating.

But the unions said otherwise: A deal's a deal. To hell with Wall Street. A political life or death struggle ensued. What lawmakers called a "hard vote" – meaning the responsible vote but one that could cost you your seat – was coming.

The unions were powerful. They had organized successfully against prominent legislators within the immediate memory of every senator or delegate. Try to pull back the COLA, the workers said, and we will end your career. No empty threat. They had, in recent memory, defeated ranking members of the assembly.

When the 1984 assembly convened, a ranking house member filed the rollback bill. Efforts to cushion the blow failed. The unions laughed. You passed it. You live with it. Every legislator understood the "or else."

The reform legislation, backed by then House of Delegates Speaker Ben Cardin (later Congressman and U.S. Senator), seemed to have enough votes to assure passage. As the session unfolded, however, the teachers and their leader, Janice Piccinini, chipped away at the numbers, leaving Cardin scrambling for the 72 votes he needed.

With only a few days remaining in the session, the bill had not been voted out of the Appropriation Committee. No bill, no reform – no AAA. A single vote was needed to break a tie and send the bill toward a vote on the House floor. Cardin and the committee chairman finally convinced a supporter of the unions to free the measure by abstaining. A no-vote gave the bill a majority. As a candidate, he'd promised to support the unions. He voted ostensibly to allow the process to move forward. He would honor his promise by voting no on the floor. No one was fooled by the maneuver.

Cardin moved quickly lest his fragile majority slip away. The vote was called and the old mechanical tally board whirled. When it stopped, the bill had failed to achieve a constitutional majority of 71 votes. The Triple-A rating was lost.

Unless.

The wiles of legislative politics and various bits of legerdemain could rescue it. First, the bill was offered for reconsideration, a second bite of the lawmaking apple as it were. Under the rules a delegate who voted no had to be recruited to call for something called reconsideration. This rule allowed a second vote on hard-fought controversial issues. It allowed such issues another chance at the law-making process to give opponents – often the House Speaker or Senate president – a second chance to win the day on crucial matters, like the Triple A rating.

But that was not the most difficult problem. Not one but two votes had to be turned. The delegate who abstained was voting no on final passage. Delegate Joe Owens of Montgomery County who never voted on reconsideration moved to the "no" side. His view: You get one chance, however important a piece of legislation may be. If you lose, you're welcome to try again the following year. A year's time would have been costly for the state.

Cardin turned then to the usual problem-solving device: money. More money for Baltimore schools persuaded two Baltimore delegates, one of whom was a teacher, to see the wisdom of making Wall Street happy.

But suddenly their votes were worth millions for their city. (This circumstance may have been a legislator's fondest dream: to become the important, deal-clinching vote on a bill of great importance. Judgeships have been awarded; bridges built; and community recreation centers constructed by those who found themselves in such bargaining posture.)

On the other side of such matters stood those legislators who almost coveted what they called "the hard vote" – the right vote versus the union vote. This group of delegates and senators welcomed any opportunity to say, "That could cost you your seat in the assembly." Save the state, save the taxpayers, or save your seat. The teachers were certain to target those legislators who opposed them.

"I know we have to have this bill," one member told me, "but I like it down here." He voted with the unions.

Another member represented those delegates who saw "the hard vote" as an opportunity to illustrate what legislating was all about ...or should be.

He voted for the reform bill and, in fact, did lose his seat. (He had supported one other difficult bill in that same year. Two hard votes turned out to be a bridge too far.)

Richard Dixon, a Democrat who had promised publicly to support the unions, abstained in the appropriations committee, moving the measure to the floor. There he voted "no." As a financial adviser, he knew the importance of pleasing Wall Street. He knew how important the bill was.

On the last day of the 1984 session, Janice Piccinini sent Bobby Neal a present. Neal had been the most important and visible proponent of passage.

The union boss's present: A large, framed photograph of the iconic (in Annapolis) Fran Obrien's, a popular legislative hangout. The picture was taken as the bar burned. Billowing smoke blanketed the entrance.

"Dear Bobby," the caption read. "Wish you were THERE."

Neall ran for the U.S. House of Representatives the following year – and lost. Among the reasons: active opposition from teachers.

44

With Pulp

As he made his way tavern-by-tavern to Annapolis, General Washington never failed to plead the case of his men. They had not been paid. Really? They bled and died, nearly starved or froze to death. And now they were getting stiffed? Yes.

There were other demands for the money. Had there been any money. The United States was born broke more or less. But, should funds be found, which creditors would be first in line? Who would be available to make the soldiers' case? Thus did General Washington, father of the country, become one of the nation's first lobbyists. He had come to Annapolis, then the nation's capital, to resign his commission. That he did, but there remained the question of soldiers' pay. Washington stepped up.

Who better?

And so it has been, with Bereano and his phalanx of lobbying colleagues. The corps evolved into a third house – a band of highly paid lawyers, some former legislators – none of them subject to recall or defeat at the polls. They had more knowledge, more relationships, than all but the most senior or powerful members. Even those who were not public service lobbyists thought of themselves, with some justification, a part of the governing system.

In my Annapolis days, the title of first among lobbying equals would have gone to Bereano. He had reshaped lobbying in his own overweight image. He would say his world was not unlike the family where everyone works for the benefit of everyone else. It was, he said, a governing system driven by personal relationships. In the case of a Bereano competitor, Gerald Evans, a federal judge, said that the General Assembly had been overcome by a "culture of corruption."

Bereano's prodigious work habits, his laughing bonhomie, always seemed to me embarrassingly overdone. I thought this before I realized that overdoing things was part of the Bereano shtick.

Under Bruce, it worked the way much of life works – with relationships in which two sides behaved something like "professional friends" with something at stake for both. (Or situations where someone just wanted a favor – a vote – that would cost him or her nothing politically.) Bruce learned and acted on idiosyncrasies, likes and dislikes. Personal habits, families, breakfast food favorites – (I kid you not) – hard work, reliability and empathy. Bruce offered full-service care.

He knew the issues in a member's home district, what the delegate could and could not vote for. His or her basic, fundamental, live or die political needs. Until forbidden by ethics regulations (passed to curb some of Bereano's ministrations), he put snacks on the seats of legislators he courted – whether he needed their votes at the time or not. Jars of peanut butter. Orange juice – with pulp for the senator son of an East Baltimore bar owner. The man wanted the pulp. Was that kind of info bankable? Could be, apparently.

You are shocked by this, I know. The whole lawmaking thing revolves around money, right? Yes and no. Bruce could help you get campaign contributions. But being there every day with creature comforts --- and advice – meant almost as much. This money was, oddly, never thought of as payoff money though it seemed to have the same importance. Campaigns were expensive. Contributions kept you in office. Bruce wanted to keep his partners – his partnerships, his "votes" – in line.

The equation was clear if officially unrecognized: I help my friends, they help me by staying in office on important committees. Bereano convinced people he cared about them, wanted to help them, had their best interests at heart. That was his job. He worked it non-stop. I had dinner with him several times over the years and watched him nod off in the salad course.

No one ever heard Bruce say no. Not a word he used. He lived with these people 10 or 15 hours a day. He knew they actually got homesick, separated from home and hearth and children. He knew the whole place seemed like 'Das Boot, too crowded, a bit stifling. Sure, you worked with history and status and some small measure of political power, also morning-after exhaustion after marathon hearings. He would step in with something to ease the occasional depression. Nothing seemed to take his attentions too far. Nothing embarrassed him or the votes he courted.

If Bereano said "nice to see you," he meant it. It was all about the votes, of course. Not just the yeses or nays. A senator or delegate might actually be referred to as a vote: what would an important "vote" likely do on an issue? That sort of reference suggested a kind of manipulation so you didn't actually hear it much. It went against the idea, nurtured by Bruce and others, that a lobbyist was the senator or the delegate's friend. The lawmaker himself as well as the public beyond Annapolis wanted to think issues were settled on the merits, not peanut butter or help with finding a good back doctor – but these were the building blocks of legislative life.

Getting a bill out of committee or, more often, arranging to have it die – that was the daily fare of Bruce and his colleagues. He had to have a personal relationship with as many "votes" as possible.

If citizens saw Annapolis, they saw it maybe once a year – unless they were working on a special issue that brought them down to parade and demonstrate on Lawyers' Mall at the foot of the State House steps in the shadow of Thurgood Marshall's almost lifelike, almost literally striding statue.

Not to suggest the issues didn't matter. They absolutely did. A senator or delegate would not be your friend if you didn't protect him or her on issues that could create enemies – a teachers' union, a business organization, a church group. You, the lobbyist, you Bruce, would be the teacher. You would always know more than the "vote." Always. You were part of the process as much as any elected representative you depended on. You would explain the fracking bill to someone from the Eastern Shore if he didn't get it. The Shore rep would want to understand why it was prudent to spend $10 million per mile of highway through the mountains. Here the lobbyist served the state itself.

One of the many public service lobbyists, Vinny DeMarco, competed with Bruce almost every year. DeMarco won almost all these fights. He was fighting to take cigarette tax money to expand the eligibility for welfare or to make smoking too expensive for children. He had developed a system that depended not on peanut butter or orange juice, but on health. In both cases, Bereano represented the other side. Tobacco interests (vending machine operators and tobacco growers) fought the tax increases.

DeMarco wondered why businesses were still willing to hire Bereano after he had gone to jail for violating the campaign finance rules.

I tried to explain; Bruce got hired *because* he had gone to jail. He was taking a bullet for his employers. They paid him handsomely for taking some issues right to the edge of legality or beyond. He was saying, in effect, I will go to jail for you. And he did.

When he was on trial for one of his alleged offenses, dozens of delegates and senators went to court to testify on his behalf. Leadership of the two houses – the House speaker and the Senate president –was not happy. They had, over the years, tightened the rules governing lobbyist's entertainment. It became more difficult to buy lunch for a "vote." Usually Bruce and his colleagues found a way around the rules. Maybe you couldn't buy lunch for one pivotal committee member, but you could if you invited them all. Every member would not come. They knew it wasn't about them.

I was to some extent an enabler. (And also, there were many times when Bruce helped me on a story.) I was like DeMarco. I didn't quite get it. Much of what I wrote showed Bruce playing right up to the edge. He couldn't have asked for better advertising.

He was eventually caught on the wrong side of the line. He went to jail. And yet, he came back to the legislature, his prowess intact. For a time, he came to hearings on his bills wearing an electronic ankle bracelet and living under a curfew that ordered him back to a half-way house by 4 p.m.

Inevitably, he had to leave some hearings early.

When his name was called one afternoon, a spokesman told the committee chair, "Mr. Bereano had a previous commitment." The chairman, knowing of Bereano's predicament, stifled a giggle.

45

The Mikes

Bereano's "relationship" approach to passing or killing bills led to gross excesses. The "votes" lived on a per deim allowance for food and lodging. But the senator or delegate might live a little higher off the hog. He or she might openly declare his or her hunt for a "sponsor" – meaning a lobbyist who had left his card with a friendly waiter or maître de along with instructions to cover so and so's tab.

That sort of blatant, public vote buying was stopped by the presiding officers. These men (always men until 2019) acted quickly to protect the process. Newspapers or legislators blew the whistles. The honor of the assembly suffered nevertheless, leading to the assertion that a culture of corruption had fallen over the lawmaking process. Usually the sponsor games were outlawed by ethics rules before taking hold and yet the disclosure produced concern that money could disrupt the process. A public race to first lobbyist to reach earnings of $1 million a year did not help, (Bereano liked to be more precise: not per year but per four-month legislative session.)

This suggestion that the legislature was out of control ended quietly under a succession of speakers, including Ben Cardin, later a U.S. Senator.

In 2003 when Michael E. Busch, an Anne Arundel County Democrat, became the House Speaker. His 16-year tenure – longest in state history – was marked by a clear message that "sponsorships" and other cozy relationships would be dealt with swiftly. Offenders would find themselves stripped of power and the virtual elimination of their ability to represent constituents. Punishment came with a tacit invitation to leave. Mike Busch made zero tolerance the rule.

I admired most of the men who ran the Senate and House. Busch more than most. I had my professional arm's length relationship with them all. With Busch it was different. There was a sports connection. But I was impressed with his determination to keep working for what he thought was the right solution – slot machine gambling being the best example. He didn't win always. But when the issue was settled and gambling came, he tried to make the best of the new reality.

He and I talked a lot about football. He'd been a pro-caliber running back at Temple. I had played at UNC when Sunny Jim Tatum was the coach. I never made the team. But we had that link. And others.

In 1988, I wrote a book about Len Bias, the University of Maryland basketball star who died of a cocaine overdose *Lefty, Lenny and the Chancellor,* Bancroft Press.). Busch read the book. He and I talked about it – and particularly a passage in the introduction where I recounted a high school football game in which I failed to catch a tipped ball. The wobbling pass hung in the air just out of my lunging reach. Occasionally when I passed him in the hall he'd smile and say, "That ball still up there?" as if I still had a chance at it.

He was the most open-to-reporters speaker in my days in Annapolis. I could get in his office and stay for as long as I wanted. Once we ran into each other at a coffee shop in Charlotte, North Carolina, during the 2012 Democratic nominating convention. We started talking again about football or basketball, I'm pretty sure he gave the whole highlight reel of his football career.

He paused at one point, smiling a self-directed smile and said, "You know the older I get the better I was." With all this personal and policy talk, I thought I had a special relationship with him. When he died in March of 2019, I saw he had a special relationship with almost everyone he worked with.

My dealings with his colleague, Senate President Thomas V. Miller – the nation's longest serving, state senate president – was usually confined to legislative business. We had our moments – some difficult, some remarkable.

I wrote a profile of him, how his mother managed to keep him enrolled at the University of Maryland over the wishes of his father. She amended his lackluster report cards so her husband wouldn't have a reason to bring him home. She ironed his shirts, tucking a few bills in the pockets so he'd have some spending money.

Based on his later political performance, his mother gave the state a remarkable leader. His skill at building and maintaining support kept him in office. He became famous for his knowledge of the state's and the nation's political history – the Civil War in particular.

On the day my profile ran, I gave him a copy of *The Killer Angels*, which, somehow, he had not read. Three years later, I ran into him in a state office building. He and others were re-drawing the state's congressional district lines. Out of the blue, he stopped to tell me how much he disliked my profile which, he suggested, I had attempted to soften with the gift or a "damned paperback book."

We had other combative encounters, but we also had periodic chats about state history. After one of these, he gave me a splendid Civil War biography written by a Marylander who served as a chaplain in the Confederate army. A lovely gilt-edged volume versus a "a damned paperback." Wonder who won that exchange.

He and Busch were not personally close in any way – until the 2019 legislative session. In January of that extraordinary year, both men set out with life-threatening health conditions.

Busch, who had prevailed over serious medical issues for several years, died of pneumonia one day before the final gavel. Miller had disclosed early in the session that he was being treated for advanced prostate cancer.

Weakened and seemingly in pain, he survived to eulogize his colleague in the House chamber, on "sine die," Latin for adjournment without return, For Busch and his mourning colleagues, of course, the parliamentary term had poignant significance.

He had worked with many governors and speakers, Miller said, but the 16-year partnership with Busch had been the most rewarding.

His own performance did not go unmentioned. Sen. Robert A. Zirkin (D-Baltimore County), chairman of the Senate Judicial Proceedings Committee: "I just want to say – on behalf of the entire Senate – how much we absolutely admire everything you're doing and everything you've done this session."

Marylanders found themselves watching the end of an era. Two proud and skillful legislators had been the rock of government for 16 years. As if nothing else could end their partnership, illness moved in on both in the same year. Busch had been speaker longer than anyone in Maryland history. Miller's thirty-three years at the rostrum set a national-record for state senate presidents.

Governors come and go. These two men, their personal ambitions apparently well-satisfied, presided over many issues of consequence. Governors worked with them, to be sure, but they built the winning margins on issues from the death penalty to gender equality to education funding.

I managed to get a seat in the House gallery to see Miller struggle into the joint session and give his eulogy.

Given Maryland's history of Democratic Party dominance, bi-partisanship meant that Busch's more progressive House and Miller's more conservative Senate – not always in sync – had reached agreement.

46

New Management

When the assembly was not in session, I had other stories to do. I wrote a color piece about the 1983 World Series in Philadelphia after the Orioles won. I wrote a long piece about the city's 250th birthday. When a policeman was killed while arresting a deranged young man at the Greyhound station, I wrote about that.

I drove to western Maryland to interview his parents who lived far enough into the mountains to remind me of the movie "Deliverance." The young man had been terrorizing his family with episodes of violent behavior. Their dog jumped up and nipped me in the chest as I was walking into their living room. What had I gotten into? The story was really about gaps in the mental health care system.

Eileen Canzian and I met while she was covering the March 1981 shooting of President Reagan. Sources directed her to a professional who knew the shooter, John Hinckley, attacked Reagan to impress the actor, Jody Foster. She further distinguished herself by convincing a priest to give her information about Congressman Robert Bauman's alcoholism – which was part of the story that Bauman had been abusing a young boy.

We were introduced, dated a bit, became an item (as they say) and married.

We agreed that, since I had three kids, we would limit ourselves to one more. That wouldn't upset the world population balance. Pregnancy followed. No real drama here. But there was one thing.

Eileen's grandfather was a twin – so, of course, it was important to know if we were in the every-other-generation twin pattern. (The *Times* says twins-run-families is a myth.)

But I interrupt myself:

I remember the sonogram moment vividly.

"Why are we here?" the young tech asked with a smile.

We explained. Just a routine check to see what was going on.

She snapped on the machine. "Yep," she said. "There's two of 'em in there."

I braced myself against the nearest wall. You're doubly blessed, we were told. Indeed. Still, I knew newborns and newspaper schedules were not entirely compatible. Twins? I don't think anyone recycled the totally incorrect idea that two are as easy to manage as one.

By then a Newspaper Guild official, Eileen drove to the paper where the union's bargaining committee was meeting. We were about to go on strike. So, Anna and Emily would eventually join their mother in an effort to find a few more dollars for our suddenly even more challenged budget. You got a few dollars from the strike fund for picketing. We should have qualified for three times the usual compensation.

As usual with twins, they were early arrivals. They were 4 pounds 10 ounces (Anna); and 3 pounds 8 ounces (Emily). They nursed every three hours for months. I began to understand why sleep deprivation was such an important part of interrogation.

At birth, they fell below the lowest point on the pediatrician's growth chart. At two, they were above the top-most point on that chart. We lived a block from the Saturday Farmers Market.

When Eileen was assigned to handle the General Assembly, I became the deadline-free parent, the one who could leave at 4:30 – 5 – to fetch the children. I happily (sort of) agreed. It was my turn. I got assigned to Perspective, the paper's Sunday analysis section.

The arrangement allowed us to avoid the difficulties of a spouse editing a spouse's stories, a circumstance thought to be perilous for both paper and marriage. No one wanted domestic conflict on deadline.

Newspaper life was not ideal for married persons. Editors, who had done the work, tended to think a reporter's wife understood that her husband would not always be home for dinner. He or she might have to do a story in some other state – or country. Part of the deal. Important work, etc., and work the reporter wanted to be doing. It was always about the story – so the spouse said, "I understand" when the inevitable separations came along. "Understand" didn't always mean OK. And there was more strain and tension in the marriage.

And sometimes the pairing worked well for the paper. In 1988, we won an Associated Press prize for a series of stories about lead paint poisoning, rampant in our old industrial city.

I became the househusband, the drop off and pick-up parent who could leave for the drive to daycare. One deadline a week for the Sunday paper. Manageable. In addition to my editing responsibilities, I tried to content myself with the odd column for the op-ed page. I hoped these pieces would be well-received; for me, it became something of a columnist tryout.

47

Computers

They didn't call him Whizz for nothing. In the 1980s, he was the *Evening Sun's* man in Washington. He was the bureau. He became the newspaper's first telecommuter. The father of young children, he wanted to see them in the evening. So he did his reporting during the day, went home at a reasonable hour. And filed his story in the morning.

How did he do that, file his story, that is? The answer illustrates the movement of newsrooms into the age of computers. He was one of those who started the move away from the linotype machine, away from the composing room – away from where we all started – to the cyber world.

He went to the local Radio Shack store and bought a small laptop computer. This was long before computers were introduced in newsrooms. The device he bought came with an instructional manual. He figured out how to hook it up with a small TV screen. He could compose on the computer with his words appearing on the screen. When finished, he could file his stories. He was able to do this because he learned how to program what needed to be programmed. He taught himself from the instruction manual, which he says was reasonably clear. A 9th grader could have done it, he says, suggesting that his colleagues might have been able to learn how to use what he had created.

It would take his colleagues some years – and it would take much patience on his part. He was the ideal teacher since he knew what reporters did and what they needed. He became one of the most important IT men in the building, advising on each new generation of machine as they were introduced. He helped management learn how to proceed more economically than they might have. He was demonstrating in grand style a fact of a newspaper reporter's world: life was one long adult education class where you learned some complicated thing every week or so. You learned how AFDC worked, how global warming worked and how computers worked.

Starting with his Radio Shack laptop, he ushered in a revolution. Or was it a Trojan horse?

48

Invasion

Along with their obnoxious assumption of superior newspapering skill, a team of new editors brought personal, political and careerist tension to the *Sun* newsroom in late 1991.

The new boys had come to save us from ourselves.

The start of the regime was promising, nevertheless. You can be a little resentful of newcomers and still hope for new energy. In late 1991, John Carroll, the new top editor in from Lexington, Kentucky, had earlier had earlier been a reporter and Vietnam war correspondent for the *Sun*. Often, it seemed, you got newsroom leadership from the copy desk, from people who'd never been on the street. Carroll had done the work.

We crowded into a meeting room for his introductory remarks. He seemed a bit nostalgic.

"I actually thought about having this job a long time ago," he said. And there he was.

My confidence rose a bit also because he and I had traced a bit of the same newspaper landscape. We both had worked for the *Providence Journal* before coming to the *Sun*. I never figured out if he was there before or after me. I know he wasn't there long. I never met him until Baltimore. He was moving fast.

One other thing: He was way too handsome to be a newspaper reporter or editor. His grey-blond hair seemed always about to fall over his eyes. He had a great smile, misleadingly friendly I discovered. Even so, as it turned out, he kept the smile in reserve for official photographs. The rest of the time it had a bit of an edge to it.

"What's new?" he would ask if you passed him or stood with him on the elevator. A common enough conversation starter. He wanted whoever he'd bump into to tell him something he didn't know. Fair enough, but a bit jarring.

He seldom asked with anything like a smile. If I didn't have something for him, I felt like I wasn't in the game. Probably the desired response. I learned later that one of my colleagues kept a list of things he was working on should that question come his way.

Maybe off-balance was the other useful result of the "What's new?" question. Didn't actually matter. You might not get a hearing even if you did have an idea. You had to start thinking like he did – not like the way you had been thinking. Nothing particularly bracing in that. We never had to do much "managing up" or guessing the boss's moods. We went in with an idea, laid it on the table and waited for a response.

In one of my first efforts with John, I said, "We should take a look at this (1980) welfare reform idea the Clintons are buying. Half of Baltimore or more is on welfare. The new thing could be pretty disruptive. Or it might work better than the critics think."

"No," he said. "Newspapers do too many process stories. If Martians landed, they would fairly conclude that nothing other than government was available for newspapers to investigate."

In retrospect, I thought he would surely be interested in the work David Simon did on police. Simon would have been the proverbial fire hose of ideas. His work was leading to a phenomenal career, first as author of "Homicide" and later "The Corner" and "The Wire" then "Treme" and on and on. He had taken a year's leave of absence to write "Homicide." When he tried to resume his *Sun* career post-"Homicide," things did not go well.

He asked for a raise.

John may have thought Simon was using his well-received book as leverage in the pay arena. Time to put him in his place?

It wasn't as if the *Sun* paid handsomely or even adequately and certainly not sufficiently high to claim all of our time. Whatever Carroll said to Simon, it wasn't "yes."

"It was like I threw a dead dog on the table," David said later.

His less than promising return was followed by his suggestion of stories about the criminal harvesting of copper piping from Baltimore's ravaged housing stock. John said "no." I don't know why that idea, which seemed a strong one to me – a city dismantled from underground by thieves – didn't get John's approval. My guess: he thought it would have produced squishy results of some value to policy makers – but soporifics for readers and contest judges.

David did the story anyway, selling it to the paper's Sunday magazine.

So, here was Simon executing an end run around his already unhappy boss. He was off soon to become an international name with "The Wire" – an extraordinary achievement (and maybe a long-range push for anti-Carroll revenge). I may have been collateral damage.

In 1999, my political biography of Mayor Schaefer was published by The Johns Hopkins University Press. John ordered the book's editor, Michael Pakenham, not to review it. Pakenham offered an explanation in his column.

Carroll, he wrote, wanted all our work for his newspaper, the *Sun*. Books about police detectives or zany political figures included. But there was no rule when I began the project or after. Nothing of the sort was ever announced as company policy.

I was so distracted by John's decision that I missed the fact that Pakenham had sneaked a very generous appraisal of my book into his regular column:

> *Smith traces Schaefer from earliest childhood through his full and complicated life. So intertwined is that with the neighborhoods, customs, social rituals – the dreams and provincialisms – of Baltimore that the book becomes an enchanting social history of Schaefer's home town almost as much as it is a tracing and interpretation of the man himself.*
>
> *Almost, but not quite. Schaefer is the heart of the tale with all his charm and all his imperfections – vulgar and pious, cruel and humane, petty and destiny-driven.*
>
> *In December 1975, Smith judges, Schaefer achieved full maturity, with his inauguration for a second term as mayor. To hold together his fractious body of supporters, Smith writes, "he had to make them confident he would never abandon them, or*

forget their needs. His only venture beyond the bread and butter of governing was his promise to make government and government programs open to all Baltimoreans."

And that he did, and then reached out to the entire state. Smith is a richly elegant, often eloquent writer. This book swims – joyfully, just like Schaefer – in affection for the human intricacies of politics and politicians, for the role in government affairs of whimsy, eccentricity, random chance, passion and cussedness.

Like Schaefer and many others who populate this book, Smith exhibits an enthusiasm for cities and their human importance that is virtually operatic. Characters emote as much as they govern. This is a saga of the experiences of local government raised to the divine, plummeted to the abysmal.

John did have some regard for my work. He ordered me back on the State House staff. He had to arrange separate editing because, otherwise, I would have been working for my wife, then handling politics and government stories. That situation might prove disrupting for both the domestic and professional situation.

When I got a tip about the identity of Deep Throat, Carroll authorized a trip to Florida to work it. The tip came from Tom O'Malley whose son Martin, was a Baltimore City Councilman, later governor of Maryland and presidential candidate.

Tom, his other son Peter and I flew to Florida to find O'Malley's boyhood friend who had become Watergate Judge John Sirica's secretary. He was in a position to know a lot, but we found the man debilitated by drinking and unable to give us anything the real Deep Throat would have known.

He did have a lovely bass voice.

Finally, I told O'Malley I didn't think this was the man.

He was not happy with me.

"I know I could convince a jury, he's the guy," he insisted. Something I had never thought of occurred to me then: your basic newspaper editor had a higher bar for convincing evidence than your basic jury or judge. So the mission failed to give us much. The *Sun* was not going to publish Tom O'Malley's circumstantial case.

I had called Bob Woodward.

"No," he said, "Not him. I think we probably talked with him but he was not the source." So the tip didn't pan out. Would've been great to find the most famous source ever. Also, would have been a good answer for Carroll's "What's new?"

49

Reporter's Rules

When we thought of succeeding, we thought of David Halberstam. So we were inclined to accept what he said about almost anything. One thing he said about a *Times* colleague, Homer Bigart, stays with me.

Bigart, he said, was in a sense, the perfect reporter.

Going in on any subject, Bigart was a blank slate. Didn't pretend to be as a tactic.

He knew nothing. Had no biases – no information or knowledge. Coming out of the assignment, he knew everything.

I heard another Homer story. He had two rules for being a foreign correspondent:

Rule 1: Don't read your stuff in the paper. Reading what the copy desk or some random editor had done to your prose would ruin your day.

Rule 2: Cheat on your expenses. We assume the second rule as stated here was tongue in cheek. But hey, Bigart was often overseas in war zones. And reporters were urged to take good care of themselves.

My friend and former editor, Jeff Price, loved to tell this story among his many others involving expenses.

Unable to add a time element to a story, Price told his editor he had no watch. The editor ordered him to get one. He did, a Rolex. When the publisher, Gary Black, came to town, he noticed:

"Nice watch," he said.

"Thanks," Price said, adding "Ought to be. You paid for it." Price had "expensed" it. In newspaperese, expense was a verb. As time went on, of course, we collected many stories about ourselves and characters we covered and, as with Bigart, our colleagues. I was told about a discussion about dinner expenses at a national party convention. It began with a question.

"Do you think," the reporter asked his boss, "it would be okay to order chateaubriand for two?" You could "expense" it, but even so, would it be okay? I think the answer was along the lines of "whatever it takes to get the work done."

We were, of course, in the business of chronicling the eccentricities of colleagues as well as subjects.

One of the yachting writers at the *Providence Journal* had an explosive temper. He was known for abusing telephones, picking them up and hurling them across the room. You had no idea what set him off.

One of his colleagues, a beat writer covering the Red Sox before they learned how to win, liked to write game stories with long quotes from the game's star. One day, Mickey Mantle of the Yankees had a remarkably productive outing. But Mantle refused to answer any questions.

Unfazed, the Journal's man started his story by reporting:

"Mantle wasn't speaking to reporters, but if he had been he would have said ..."

In political coverage you ran into equally colorful players. One of the most famous was Baltimore mayor Thomas D'Alesandro – old Tommy by the time I got to Baltimore. He knew how to deal with us. You couldn't always print what he said, but you always had to ask. Your "desk" sent you out to ask questions and that's what you did.

One day, one of my predecessors, Frank Somerville, began by saying, "Mr. Mayor, my desk wants me to ask ..." as Somerville was finishing, D'Alesandro put his head down, ear to his own desk.

"My desk," he said, "wants your desk to go fuck itself." Somerville had chosen the "my desk" dodge to ease the discomfort of asking the mayor about large expenditures for office furnishings.

And of course, there were stories I didn't write and should have: When I arrived in the Annapolis State House press room at the end of the Marvin Mandel saga. I should have written about the poem. The governor who had gone to jail for various offenses, including, finally, failure to give the people of Maryland fair and honest government.

The story I found cried out for telling. My colleagues didn't see it. And they feared becoming part of the story – though they were anyway. I'd been urged to write about what I saw first on a new assignment. After the second day even the best stuff became wall paper. The Mandel trial had gone on for so long. And yet there it was, a telling new take on the press room bulletin board, a bit of telling texture that told more than it seemed to about him and us.

A "poem":

> "Involved" by Marvin (Buddy) Mandel
> "I'm not involved.
> I was not involved in any of that.
> I know no one who was involved in any of that.
> I never would have been involved in something like that."

The story might have gone on to describe Mandel's meerschaum pipe-driven way of deflecting questions. A pipe always needed cleaning, particularly when you wanted to avoid getting involved.

We were proud of our ability to find and tell stories. One of my favorite newspaper words was "work." You worked a story. You worked a tip. Everything you did, every question from every reluctant source, every idea or angle you had, every carefully formulated question came under the heading of "working it." Some people were, it seemed, innately talented. Some were just pretty straightforward. No mystery. Just the question. That was the job, of course,

One year when he was working for the *Providence Journal,* the truly great Ben Bagdikian was somehow moved to contact the Dali Lama, then fending off some threat or other. Bagdikian asked the newspaper's operator get the man on the phone in Tibet.

After a few minutes, she called Bagdikian back.

"Do you have a street address for Mr. Lama?"

50

Not Even Close

In a certain sense, writing is an extended homage to... imperfections.

Jhumpa Lahiri, *In Other Words*

I spent my working life, as the novelist Lahiri had, trying to minimize imperfection. Of course, I failed every day. There was a small irony here. Newspapers were in business to find and expose imperfections in the work of others, even as we failed every day in ours.

Still, perfection was the goal. That's why there were so many layers of editors: copy editors, Page 1 editors, national and foreign editors, bureau editors, metro and city and managing editors and assistant managing editors. Ideally, every editor would see every story before it landed in the newspaper. One of them, at least, would find the imperfections and fix them. Or, as many as possible,

We took no solace in knowing that tomorrow offered another opportunity to get it right. Imperfection was the newsperson's rock of Sisyphus. We labored up the hill every day only to find the stone had rolled back down over night.

Discouraging, perhaps, but you did have another day. A blessing and a curse. Every one of these editors wanted an error-free newspaper. That meant stories with no unanswered questions; complete understanding of everything we printed; every person accurately named, quoted accurately with every name spelled correctly with the right middle initial. We were middle-initial fanatics.

I left them out in the *Providence*. They formalized and stilted the prose, got in the way of "the read." You wanted the story to have as much momentum as possible. You didn't want to be the source of interruption, however brief.

Even totally committed to the goal of perfection, even when you had all the editors on your side, you had to worry what I called "the lede elf'" would find a way into your story.

Of course, my colleagues and I were always the agents of imperfection. And I thought, in my own defense, some invisible agent (entirely imaginary) would sneak something embarrassing by me, into the first and most important paragraph of a story that was read by every one of these officious editors – there to be discovered by readers who would say "well, if they can't get a middle initial right, can they get anything else right?" There were no insignificant imperfections. Were we anal? Were there more important things to worry about? Yes and yes.

Of course, I learned to live with imperfection. Didn't make me happy, but I had no choice. The newspaper came out every day and would do so, I thought, forever. What I failed to perfect could be grappled with the next day. Which is not to say we took the daily-ness of the paper as a built-in bailout. The story had to be as good and as complete as it could be every day. First class, first day was the goal.

Often, we couldn't reach it. Readers knew. Movies and books talked about what an editor did when he knew he didn't have everything by deadline.

"Go with what you've got." You gave your readers "the best available version of the truth." The somewhat macho declaration got into the public domain. I imagined people smirking a bit: "Go with what you got" meant going with something less than good, less than perfect. It was too easy but what choice did you have?

I know sometimes you had to follow that dictum. Particularly on a moving story of great interest, we had an obligation to tell people everything we knew as soon as we knew it — much more so now in the age of the 24-hour news cycle. Twitter and everything else that drives media create omni deadlines. Every second or fraction of a second is a deadline.

The lifetime of a story, though, did not fit neatly into one day's reporting and deadlines. You didn't know what happened next until it happened.

I knew this. But I sweated what I didn't have. Because I knew some editor would demand I get the answer. So I kept calling, kept trying to think of someone who might know something helpful, another avenue to travel for the information. Editors did not want to hear why you couldn't answer an important question. They always thought there must be another call you could make.

I hated that tension. Even when it drove the process to the point of going with what we had, I walked away from editors, muttering about what idiots they were. They pushed. They did the hangdog thing. Then they started over.

"Give it another shot. Maybe the guy (the one with the answers) was out to dinner. Maybe he's back."

The pressure was coming from the fact that the story was now the editor's as much as it was mine. The demand for more calls could run on past the first deadline. An incomplete story was a major imperfection. Glaring. Embarrassing.

"He might be asleep?

"So what? Wake him up."

A line editor knew the story would go through the hands of higher-up editors. They would have the same questions your editor had.

"Why don't we know this or that? Did we call so and so?"

Ultimately, I banked on the knowledge and belief that each of these second-guessers had been in my position. They would eventually back off. They had confidence that if you didn't get the answer it wasn't getable. Not then at least.

The "process" would be adjusted from time to time but, to me, it seemed the adjustments were always minor, unseen and after some brief announcement left to run on their own. "System" and "process" had been adjusted if not perfected over such a long time. "Best practices" were in place or you weren't working for a good paper.

Ill-considered change brought unforeseen difficulties in a system that had no room for error. A reliable, consistent system left the participants free to exercise judgment.

Judgment. I loved the word. I hoped it would characterize my work and my newspaper's work. I suspect none of us had good judgment from birth. Judgment and insight and perspective came from experience, careful observation, listening and from colleagues who had done the work. Standards came to be inherent in the process.

I saw that even more clearly when I started covering politics. I marveled at people who thought they could run for office with no experience. Experience gave you a way to calculate odds of success and a better shot at making smart decisions — like when to run, when to wait, how to accumulate what you needed to do whatever good things you had in mind. Your first job was to win. If you had to catch lightning in a bottle you probably weren't going to get far.

51

Enemy of the People

> *You could be in the most protected place in Vietnam and still know that your safety was provisional, that early death, blindness, loss of legs, arms, or balls, major and lasting disfigurement – the whole rotten deal could come in on the freakyfluky as easily as in the so-called expected ways...*

Michael Herr, *Dispatches*

Timberg lost his face. Four hundred gallons of gasoline exploded under the jeep he was driving.

He survived to hear himself described as "The Burn." The most visible manifestation of who he was, was gone.

No bit of cloth – a shirt sleeve, a pant leg – could hide the horror.

Thirty-seven surgeries left him with a hideous calling card.

Practicalities arose as the pain eased. What could he do back in The World to make his post-war life less a trial for himself and the people he met.

"You can write," his wife told him. The proof was there in his letters.

Casting about for something that made sense, she said, "Maybe you should try newspapers."

Any profession, of course, would demand finding a way around the initial shock encountered by every new person he met. Newspaper reporting? Even more meetings with people who hadn't seen him.

In his first assignments, when there was no time to reassure anyone, he moved ahead as if people would find a way – or not. That would be their problem.

A Naval academy grad, he knew Annapolis. He hooked on with the *Annapolis Capital* and then with the *Evening Sun* in Baltimore.

Eventually, we found ourselves competing in Washington, quietly eager to beat each other. A member of Congress had fallen into a situation that could the end of a promising career. The accusation involved misuse of government funds.

One day we chased an element of the story into the suburbs of Washington, D.C. Stories filed, we stopped at a burger joint.

The facts were known by then. We talked about the big picture. Why would someone have taken such a gamble? And why, having been found out, had the questionable behavior continued? So much to lose.

Timberg said his own personal way of assessing people in trouble began with how they dealt with it. Did they own it? Were they honest about it? Did they look for excuses or scapegoats?

Reporters weren't always able to push for this sort of explanation. "Did you or didn't you?" was often the end of it. No further questions were allowed. There was no opportunity to ask them. The story played out, for good or ill. It wasn't a perfect system, reporting. Maybe you could get the whole story in a longer piece in which people who knew would help.

We were treading lightly around an essential aspect of the work we did and who we were.

We never talked about the war and its toll. How had he dealt with all of that? My two-day in and out Vietnam experience: His scars and skin grafts.

Surgeons had saved him by smoothing away 25 years of facial geography, the tracings of his life. Had his personality, there in the creases and smile-lines, been sculpted away? I knew they had not. He had saved all of it to be shown over time.

In a way, it was easier for him than for us. He had watched a new face come together one surgery at a time. He knew others would have no break-in period. At a memorial service, his daughter remembered being befuddled when playmates recoiled. What was the matter with them? It was just her father. She and her brothers and sister laughed a bit when she spoke at the service.

He had made it easier. He met the world as if the scars were beside the point. He would live the way everyone lived.

He loved to laugh. He had, somehow, a great smile. People would get it even if they wondered how someone so grievously wounded could ever – laugh. But then you found yourself laughing with him.

No one could think of this wounding as a gift. He would have had other opportunities to make a life. But here was something floating in out of nowhere.

He began to report and write. He was good at it. He won a coveted Neiman Fellowship to Harvard. He wrote a book about five of his Academy classmates. *The Nightingale's Song*, he knew, reminded plebes that serving America in the military was a gift. Broad opposition to the Vietnam War had made service in that war almost a crime for some. Then President Reagan's assertion that Vietnam was a noble cause reactivated the nightingale's song in a different way for each man. (I thought of Joe Nimiroski, war scholar Marine who became one of the first casualties from Massachusetts.)

I never got Timberg's take on it. Something told me that territory was beyond our comfort zone. Beyond mine at least.

In his memoir, *Blue Eyed Boy*, Timberg remembered the moment he decided to live through pain and disfigurement. He refused to miss knowing what the rest of his life might hold for him. He refused to be cheated.

He died at 76. On the way to his memorial service, I remembered the dinner we'd had. I had wondered that night if his story about dealing with trouble had been an invitation to talk about his own struggle. I hadn't been strong enough or brave enough to find out.

In the funeral chapel, I saw a photo of him at 22. There was no reconciling that face with the face I knew. Pat Ferguson, a Marine and Timberg's boss for a time at the *Sun*, called his life a tribute to the Corps: moving straight ahead, seeking no easy flanking maneuvers.

Timberg had no choice as "the burn." Straight ahead was the only way.

And he needed help, surgeons to give him the opportunity for a life.

But what kind of life would it be? That would be his work, his gift to himself and to us.

52

The Memorial

I had covered many anti-war rallies: Attleboro, Boston, Providence, the March on the Pentagon, Dover, Delaware, where the bodies came home (not a rally of course), Central Park.

In 1967, when I was in New York, I remember ducking into an old friend's apartment on Fifth Avenue to write my story. My lede was something like this: Doves and others of like feather, spread their wings in unison to say "No more." I hoped I wasn't spreading my own wings – announcing my own anti-war feelings. I vaguely remembered that birds of a feather had an anti-communist origin – not something I wanted to agree with or oppose. Anti-war forces were called doves. That was their derivation. There was a deadline, of course. So no time to reconsider and rewrite. Alert copy editors saved me innumerable times over the years. Not this time. As far as I know no reader complained.

In the *Providence Journal* newsroom my colleagues and I had been assiduously neutral, though I have no doubt we opposed the war. And we did notice our editorial page was remarkably strident in its criticism of Washington and Johnson.

I heard a telling story. Even as his newspaper was becoming remarkable for its opposition, the newspaper's publisher, John C.A. Watkins, was confronted one day at the Hope Club, a Yankee retreat on College Hill.

It went something like this: "Hey John, you boys are making quite an anti-war statement. You're sounding pretty dovey."

Watkins' response: "We are?"

Apparently, he had not been reading his own newspaper's editorials. One of the writers, Jim Brown, had done most of these pieces. Brown had written after Dr. King's daring anit-war speech at the Riverside Church in New York City. Anyone who didn't see why King would have chosen to step outside his civil rights focus, didn't understand King or the civil rights struggle or the war.

Someone else was put in charge of newspaper's war edits. As a salve to his pride, Brown was given a signed column. He became even more strident. Then he was fired. Management said it was his tone, not so much what he had to say, that ended his *Journal* employment. He was almost immediately hired by the *New York Times.*

Opposition on the street grew. I rode down to Washington for the March on the Pentagon with Brown University students. Two or three of them were arrested and lodged in a jail in Occoquan, Virginia. One of the Brown students, David Kertzer, ran into Noman Mailer there while he awaited bailing out. Mailer's subsequent book was titled *Armies of the Night.*

The October, 1967, rally was important enough to warrant a visit from the *Times'* Scotty Reston, then the best-known U.S. newspaper columnist. The event, he wrote, had no impact. Washington would not be dissuaded in its prosecution of the war. Reston was giving us a view of the Establishment. I think he missed the deeper story. A profound change then underway in our country. People in the street mattered. As the conflict raged, body bags mattered.

Joe Nimiroski and Valerie mattered.

Statues and memorials offer no balm or succor. This one, a measure of honor delayed. Thousands of Joe Nimiroski's and their families were recognized, finally, for their willingness to fight and die for their country. Maya Ying Lin's memorial design seemed smaller than I remembered. I'd been there to report on its unveiling. Smaller but dramatic. Its cavalcade of names reaching an apex within view of the Lincoln and Washington monuments spoke of sacrifice in a way I thought should be telling for leaders who find themselves sending young men into battle. At 4.5 million visitors every year, it stands in annual number of visitors second only to the Lincoln.

On a website where family and friends can record their own personal memorials, Valerie remembered Joe as a caring and loving person. At the time she wrote, she was living on Cape Cod. I tried but failed to reach her.

"For 46 years," she said, "Christmas has never been the same."

Donald Adams, a Vietnam vet and volunteer docent at the memorial had friends with names on the wall. I met him there one very warm October day in 2017. I had meant to visit the wall again for some time. I had written a story about the wall's dedication in 1996.

I hadn't had time on that day to find Joe's name. Now I did. I wondered if Alice and Tim and Valerie had been there. And probably others from Attleboro.

I had not met Joe Nimiroski at all and yet I had.

Donald Adams helped me find his name near the apex of the memorial's V, 4 feet above my head. Cpl. Joseph E. Nimiroski, one name among thousands and yet elegantly etched as if done for him alone.

I told Adams the story of Joe and Valerie. There must have been many like it, I said.

"Every story I ever heard from the war's survivors was different," he said. But, yes, there were parallels.

"Some guys got married right out of boot camp," he said. "Some got married in Hawaii on R&R (rest and recuperation)."

Following on naturally from these unions, he said, many soldiers had children they never knew, never saw.

"My hooch mate," Adams said, "was killed five weeks before his son was born." Did Joe and Valerie have children? I wasn't able to find her. But surely the toll goes beyond the names you see on a monument.

Senator John Kerry's question offered an enduring epitaph: "How do you ask a man to be the last man to die for a mistake?"

Or the first.

53

Sun Lies

... He was never known to make a mistake... George Morrow's mastery of all the different kinds of information that a newspaper man needs was really astonishing, and he was always adding to his stock. The Sun's *high reputation for accuracy in his day was largely due to his vigilance.*

H.L. Mencken, *The Sunpapers of Baltimore*

He stood across the street from the *Sun* at the corner of Centre and Calvert Streets, holding a metal sign not much bigger than a license plate.

Who was he? George Morrow's ghost?

On one side, the sign read: "*Sun* Errors"

On the back:

"*Sun* Lies" (After many years on the street, the sign read "Still lies," in case you didn't get it.)

A four-word stab in the heart of the newspaper and its reporters, including me. I may have taken him too seriously. But I don't think so. His message, uncontested by his target – my newspaper – found us wanting in the basics of what we did and had done since the 1837 founding: getting it right. Accuracy was the bottom line of everything. Had always been the goal at least. He was actually on the street before and after I arrived in 1977.

The newspaper did not contest his assertions. Didn't he have a right to say his piece? As a matter of policy: The *Sun* offered no rebuttal to silent or flamboyant critics. Would have looked silly. We had the presses. We had the power. We had professionals gathering the news and writing it. What did this man have aside from his little sign? The newspaper's employees shouldn't be out on the street grappling with unhappy readers. Our product, our performance had to be our defense.

The policy ran through everything. We printed erroneous or misguided letters to the editor with the same very fair (we thought) attitude. We printed what they said no matter how much we disagreed. People were to get their shots at us. And of course, there were many.

Mencken, I am told, had a stock response to critics:

"Dear Sir (or Madam)

"You may be right…"

So, the man on the corner was nailing us with wicked ease. We were not untouchable, not free to err or to lie without fear of protest.

A flip of the wrist:

"*Sun* Lies"

"*Sun* Errors"

Over and over – with a wide smile at every flip.

He kept at it. In time, he developed an explanation leaflet for anyone who asked. He insisted he was picketing out of principle – a demand for accuracy – and not for profit. People began to wonder if he was all there. We wrote stories about him and the offense he felt. But after a while he became part of the outdoor wallpaper. Except for newcomers, no one at the newspaper noticed him after a while. Might have been true among the car-borne passersby as well.

What accounted for him and for my reaction to him? First, I thought: Maybe it's just the freedom to do it. Maybe he likes thumbing his nose at the big, untouchable newspaper, standing out there, Everyman enjoying his freedom of speech.

"Nobody is too big to be humble," he told one of the reporters who chronicled his campaign.

Might have been a bit of that in the mix. But here's the story, I discovered later (from stories by my colleagues):

His name was Rudolph Handel. The name made him seem a bit Old World and musical. (He was picketing after all just down the street from the

Peabody Conservatory of Music.) He stood like a one-man Messiah in search of retribution. He had made a career of it, motivated by success.

A set of false teeth didn't fit as he thought they should, so he picketed his dentist, walking away eventually with a new set.

He was onto something, or thought he was.

Not too long after that, he went after an appliance store for selling, he said, a bad TV. The store moved.

Years later, I think, I was reminded of Jay Spry, the epic re-write man in Russell Baker's book *Good Times*. Burning roof tiles had fallen on a car in a Baker story. Had burning roof tiles ever fallen on the man's car before? Spry wanted to know. A reporter might have thought the question silly. But wouldn't the story have been better if it had happened before.

Likewise, if you didn't ask Handel about his picketing, you might not have gotten an important part of his tale. We had a serial protester here, a man making his mark in the world by refusing to take the world's various affronts in silence. Or maybe he was just a crank. You weren't going to know if you didn't ask.

Handel was getting no satisfaction from the *Sun*. Or was he? The cars and their passengers were his audience. I guess he thought they would be sympathetic, and some were in a knee-jerk way. He reminded me of the cartoonist Al Capp's Joe Btfspik, a man with a dark cloud following him everywhere. Joe was always frowning. Handel smiled.

I heard that what upset him about the *Sun* had been addressed. But the correction or clarification or whatever it was, had, he said, contained another error. This must have sustained him. "See what I'm telling you?" He seemed to be saying.

He continued his campaign for 17 years. Somewhere during his long career, he switched to a more elegant version of the sign, this one made of wood.

He lived in a hotel for the elderly, faithfully manning his post (except in rain) throughout those years, racking up thousands of hours. He was found dead one morning when hotel staff realized they hadn't seen him for a while. His signs were there in the room with him.

Part IV:

Less

With Less

54

Bloody Tuesday

Under the big picture editorship of John Carroll, The Sun redoubled its coverage of the Chesapeake Bay. Carroll persuaded the nonpareil Tom Horton to come back from his many book enterprises to embarrass our *Washington Post* brethren with his depth of knowledge and his elegant prose.

Every sacred coverage area – every story – had to have high caliber reporting and editing. Carroll thought newspapers tended to over-cover politics and governments. Still, he wanted every political story as well. We would flood the zone – the Maryland General Assembly, the Orioles, Congress, the Bay – with as many reporters as we could afford. The austerely imposing Johns Hopkins Hospital with a statue of Christ in the lobby and the state's outbreak of political corruption were our seed corn. We had to own them.

Competition mattered. We had to be beating the *Post*. We were losing reporters and editors but so were they then. (A few years later, the august Watergate-breaking paper was sold for $250 million to Amazon's awesomely wealthy Jeff Bezos. Not every paper would find a savior. The *Post* found two: Bezos and Donald Trump, whose Presidency gave the *New York Times* and the *Post* tens of thousands of new subscribers.)

Papers like the *Sun*, one of those fabled "backbone of democracy papers," were not so fortunate. The first signs of Internet-generated change were upon us but imperceptibly. One year on the short road to financial collapse, at the annual building-wide, state-of-the-paper assembly, we got what should have been alarming news:

The paper was in the black only because the cost of newsprint (the paper newspapers are printed on) had gone down. We were leaning against the thinnest of reeds.

I don't remember anyone remarking on this factoid. I didn't spend much time worrying about it either. And then the full catastrophe – plant-wide layoffs – was upon us, it seemed, overnight. Why hadn't we seen it coming? We hadn't been telling our own story – not even to ourselves. No wonder our readers tended to think we were in good health. We always had been. We wrote somewhat mournfully about end times at Beth Steel. Don't cry for us. *We're* bullet-proof, permanent.

And then we were terminal. Staff cuts looked to ownership like the way to retain profitability or to break even. Was there any talk of finding a sweet spot between cuts and loss of quality? None I heard of.

The cuts were deep. I imagined a newsroom full of people with dollar signs on their backs: $65,000, here $70,000 there. If you were hemorrhaging ad revenue and subscribers, if you were looking at years of recovery at best, the way to stay afloat was through the newsroom – or the editorial office – or elsewhere in the building. Editors and reporters were not merely numbers – then they were.

Eileen, my ex-wife, lived in dread of layoff conversations. She worried for reporters with little seniority, that decisions would be made without her. One day you were putting out a newspaper, thinking about play and art -- and then end-times were on your mind.

Mary Corey, the newspaper's first and only woman managing editor, walked up behind Eileen's desk around 5 in the afternoon one day.

"Come back to my office," she said.

Swine flu had touched down on the Eastern Shore of Maryland. Corey would be eager to know what angle the paper would choose. Eileen was ready for that discussion. But the meeting wasn't about the Sunday paper.

"Times are tough," Corey began as if an editor at the *Sun* needed that information. But more discussion of the paper's condition followed. Corey kept talking. Okay, and...

"I suddenly realized what was coming. She was laying *me* off. "

"Nothing personal. Not about your work," Corey said. "Things are really bad."

"I never thought they would lay me off," Eileen said.

I did.

No one was safe. We were all numbers – not editors, not "really good" reporters. Not anything but means to immediate ends. No one illustrated the reality more than Canzian.

A Columbia Journalism school grad who had worked for Jack Anderson, the legendary investigative reporter, Canzian was a staff favorite. She could quickly assess story structure, spot unanswered questions, suggest fixes and move on to the next project. On longer, complicated stories, even the most experienced reporter gets "lost in the weeds." She could find the tunnel as well as the light. And now she was finding where the newspaper was headed. She was not the only victim of the blind-siding.

The *Sun's* green-eyeshade types eyed the op-ed page. Did we really need it? The editorial page editor said, of course, of course we need it. She arrived one morning with a proposal for saving it.

"Don't even start," she was told as she walked into the publisher's office. The page couldn't be saved, she was told. In fact, he said, the paper couldn't afford to keep her. She had arrived a few years earlier with ownership's approval. We were cannibalizing ourselves.

And this time, the damage was bone deep, an assault on systems in place for decades, the heart of the paper. There had been suggestions from the publisher's direction that editors were really not needed. Professional reporters could edit their own stories. We had gone to sleep and awakened in bean counter land, the newsroom's title for the business side. These sharp pencil people had been 0-for-life versus the newsroom – until then. Could you really have a newspaper without editors?

Suddenly, the operational infrastructure of the paper was being dismantled. The well-tested necessity of having two or even three sets of professional eyes on a story before it was published disappeared with a nothing personal, nothing professional benediction. Eighteen other editors heard the same script that day: "We have to let you go. Nothing personal. You're not the only one."

Eileen and other editors had been working on stories. Leave them, they were told.

But I have to finish .... Leave.

We had instant culture clash.

Corporate managers apparently feared editors would trash their computers if allowed to absorb their new jobless status in the newsroom. The idea that editors would feel professionally (and personally) bound to finish apparently did not occur to them.

The *Sun's* newsroom carnage was on the street instantly.

A reporter at the *Daily Record,* a legal and business newspaper, called for confirmation and comment.

Still reeling, Canzian was ready.

"If the *Baltimore Sun* doesn't think it needs my skills, experience and knowledge as an editor, it's not a place I want to be. It clearly has changed into something else."

The next morning, techies, aggregators and others came to sit in the vacated editors' chairs. The remaining reporters were told journalism had changed.

They knew.

55

Freddy Gray, Invisible Man

On April 27, 2015, Baltimore Congressman Elijah Cummings spoke at Freddy Gray's funeral. He scanned the overflow audience at New Shiloh Baptist Church: the white casket, the grieving Gray family and the picket line of 30 or 40 TV cameras in the balcony.

"As I thought about the cameras," Cummings said as he stood, "I wondered, Did anybody recognize Freddie when he was alive? Did anyone see him?" Outside the black community, he meant.

Did anyone know he had been a junior usher in his church? Did anyone know he played football for the Sandtown Wolverines?

Did anyone know of him beyond his record of criminal justice involvement?

The church sanctuary erupted in appreciation of Cummings' questions, questions aimed at the world of critics who never saw Gray or Trayvon Martin or any of the other black men dead at the hands of police willing or eager to subdue them with chokeholds or guns.

The congressman had been on the street every night of the Gray uprising. One of the most important Democratic congressmen, Cummings lives in Sandtown-Winchester, one of the poorest, debilitated neighborhoods probably in the country, the neighborhood where Gray grew up.

In this week of tension and turmoil, Cummings drove to Washington every day. His House committee on Oversight and Government Reform was holding another hearing on the Benghazi affair. The sharecropper's grandson had become chief defender of Hillary Clinton, who was Secretary of State when the American ambassador and three others were killed in a raid on the U.S. diplomatic compound there.

Cummings made a Benghazi to Baltimore daily round trip, on international and home base significance.

"Let's go home," he urged. "We're here because we love you."

A young man, 16 or so, approached him.

"Mr. Cummings," he said, "sometimes I feel like I'm in my casket clawing to get out."

Sandtown-Winchester kids like Gray struggle against long odds. Unemployable men, men with criminal records, men with families to support have little or no opportunity for jobs. They and their families live amid elevated rates of chronic conditions – diabetes, heart disease, cancer and lead paint poisoning.

I vaguely remembered that the city health department published these statistics. Their report rather matter of factly said life expectancy in this largely black neighborhood was 5 years shorter than in largely white Charles Village, a few blocks to the north and east.

How could any of us be living in a city with this damning profile, I wondered, live with it, not know about it, never speak of it or do anything about it?

The newspaper, my old newspaper, had given it insufficient attention. The *Sun's* staff was down 75 percent from circa 2008. In the past, a reporter with the poverty beat would have covered this for the daily or used it as "string" – information – for stories planned for down the road. A good reporter would have known what Cummings was pulling together with Jay Perman, president of the University of Maryland, Baltimore. A poverty beat reporter, had there been one, might have written an advance and then a daily story on the event – particularly given the Freddie Gray prologue.

A year before the Gray tumult, in the spring of 2014, the university had openings for 25 city students for its long-running internship program. In a city of 630,000 with a school system of 185,000, the university said it could not find 25 qualified kids.

Really? What were they looking for? 25 Stephen Hawkings?

Congressman Cummings called Perman with a fury Perman remembered for years.

"You can't find 25 black kids? Are you kidding me?" the congressman shouted, or words to that effect. "I can find them right outside your door. You want to come with me right now?"

Perman's office overlooks Martin Luther King Jr. Boulevard a kind of gateway – and barrier – to the West Baltimore area where "The Wire" was filmed. Cummings calls it "the inner-inner-city." Realtors were known to steer home buyers away from these streets.

To be fair, Perman had decried this kind of negative thinking. He wanted safe streets where his employees could live safely and walk to work. And he had wanted the special program to continue.

The congressman and the university president began to meet regularly.

Cummings' fury came out of personal experience – out of his life in Baltimore and his life as a member of the U.S. Congress. This son of South Carolina sharecroppers had been warned away from law school by a high school guidance counselor.

You'll never be a lawyer," the counselor said. "Don't even think about it." He thought about it. He used it as a spur.

His mother helped him.

"There are a lot of educated fools in the world," she told him.

"She had a third-grade education," he said, "but a Ph.D. in common sense."

Consigned to "special education" as a grammar schooler, Cummings went to City College, Coppin State College (1969) and the University of Maryland School of Law (1973). He won election to the Maryland House of Delegates, serving 14 years, and then to the Congress of the United States (1996),

Cummings' anger and Perman's embarrassment led to an expanded program for young people without assets or allies. The university was able to win support from the National Cancer Institute. Maryland had the first hyper-intense STEM program for 6th and 7th graders. The so-called CURE program had never before reached into grammar schools. Perman urged earlier efforts to prepare kids for healthcare fields.

For Cummings, the death of Freddie Gray in 2014 – by accident, by police brutality, by neglect – became a grievous illustration of his argument for programs like the one he and Perman engineered. Gray's death might have been predicted for him at birth. And, of course, it had been by statistics: endemic illegal drug use and sale, the high number of virtually unemployable felons, school drop outs and exposure to chronic disease.

But to most of us, Gray was invisible, as invisible as when Ralph Ellison wrote *Invisible Man*. To be sure, the *Sun* had a strong record of attention to these inner-city ills. What was needed was a new approach, a new way to promote political action. The loss of staff made simply keeping up difficult.

The *Sun's* police reporting of the Gray death and the conflagration that followed was exemplary. Its reporters on the street and its editorial writing were recognized as second best in the nation by the 2016 Pulitzer committee, which gives awards every year for the best work of newspapers.

In the fall of 2015, a few months after the Gray uprising, the Cummings-Perman program got underway – not with 25, but with 44 boys and girls from neighborhoods across the Martin Luther King Jr. highway.

Two objectives were met: Inner city students would get started on productive, well-paying careers – and they would work in medical laboratories addressing health care disparities between blacks and whites.

"Let's get these kids on track to be scientists or physicians or researchers," Perman said. "Let's get them ready to work at our Bio Center." Until then many minority workers typically cleaned bathrooms, cut the grass or clipped hedges.

At the program's opening ceremony, Cummings gave a version of his Freddie Gray funeral oration:

"Thank you, Dr. Perman, for seeing our kids. Thank you Cancer Society and thank you city of Baltimore for this wonderful program."

"Freddie Gray," he said, quoting the black national anthem, "was born in a time when hope unborn had died." Perhaps change would come as Sam Cooke had promised for the next generation of Sandtown kids.

Now there was CURE – a bureaucratic name for giving inner city kids a way to qualify for professional careers in health care and health sciences.

The university's main hall was filled with parents and teachers and friends eager to see otherwise invisible children in white lab coats emblematic of this pathetically overdue effort.

The program, the event, the National Cancer Institute, the kids in their coats could not have been more important for a suffering, still violent city. Many good programs by many other individuals and institutions were underway in Baltimore. But many of them were as invisible as Freddie Gray. The city needed a tonic. It needed something to help it past the pain of poverty and death in the streets.

The *Sun* did not cover the event.

It had become one of the nation's best newspapers – still admirable, struggling to maintain its reputation. In the previous 15 years, one in five American newspapers had gone out of business. Survivors had become what researchers call "ghost newspapers"- mere shells. Many of them had become products – no longer well-staffed, aggressive watchdogs and standard bearers of civic life and culture. They had tried to stay alive as a product – their historic mission out of reach.

Cummings and others had predicted a loss of media interest when the cameras left. Nothing was burning. There were no cops in riot gear, no looters, no sirens – no cameras.

A university president, a congressman and a national cancer fighting institution – not to speak of 44 inner city kids who had won the equivalent of the lottery – were enough to merit coverage. Missed stories like this one illustrate a newspaper's wider importance. Citizens need to know society still has the power and determination to strive for a better world. Hope lived in Baltimore but did it really if no one knew?

56

The Printers' Mass

In 2013, the last printers' Mass was said in Baltimore. Nothing showed the history – or the future – of newspapers in Baltimore more clearly.

Early in the previous century, an editor at one of the *Sun's* competitors, the *News American*, grew concerned about the drinking and gambling he saw among his men. He asked a parish priest to raise the issue with diocesan officials. Masses were permitted then only after dawn and before noon on Sundays unless the Holy Father granted an exception. Would the Bishop ask the Vatican for what amounted to a relaxation of church law? Newspapers had the standing to make such a request.

A looser schedule of Masses had been desired more generally in the diocese, but the needs of newspaper men and newspapers provided a practical reason. A 12:15 a.m. service would fit nicely with the end of the Saturday night shift. The printers would no longer have to contemplate going home for a few hours before rising to meet their holy obligations. There may have been no more than a few hundred craftsmen, but their request was granted

It was a meaningful favor. The special Mass became a part of the culture. Both papers were within a five-minute walk of the designated church, St. Vincent de Paul at the corner of North Front and East Fayette Streets. A parish of the well-to-do in the 1800s, St. Vincent's was becoming in the early 1900s a portal for immigrants. A wave of Irish was followed by one of Italians. The church, with its elegant three-stage white dome, was virtually across the street from Little Italy.

The pressmen, it turns out, were in the vanguard of something on the order of more liberal church law. A newspaper editor's request turned out to anticipate the desires of many more Baltimoreans.

The city had been a haven for free black Americans since the mid-1800s and for southern blacks who moved to the city during the Depression. The 1880 census counted approximately 6 percent free "colored persons" and about the same number of slaves. Worshipers from the St. Vincent's parish and beyond saw great convenience in the new hours. Soon after the 12:15 a.m. Mass, a 2:30 a.m. service was added.

Four years later, in 1916, Pastor Philip B. McGuire offered special Lenten Masses at noon for downtown office workers and businessmen who wanted to pray on weekdays in late winter and spring. Word spread. As many as 1,400 came to the weekend service for some years. The church's bank account grew.

"The printers' Mass became part of the fabric of the city, part of what made Baltimore tick," the Rev. Richard T. Lawrence, St. Vincent's pastor observed in 2013. "We were pleased to be a part of it."

He says the printers' Mass inadvertently came to the aid of young men on their way home – late – with dates. They could take strides toward absolution from furious fathers if they showed up with a program from the Mass.

"Saved my life a couple of times," said the priest. Fathers knew there was no traffic so that excuse was gone. But if a lad could show he'd been in church... Father Lawrence imagined the young woman's father saying to himself: "I guess I'll let him live."

The printers opened the way for communicants of every stripe. When the 2:30 a.m. service was offered, strippers and bartenders and others from The Block walked over in search of quieter contemplation. Individual sport fishermen, heading out early stopped on the way for the printers' Mass. Policemen and firemen were regulars as well.

Inevitably, the odd inebriate arrived. Over time, some people referred to this midnight service as "the drunkard's Mass." Father Lawrence says one of his predecessors stood at the top of the steps scanning the would-be congregants. His orders: "If they can walk up the stairs let 'em in. If not, throw 'em out." Just the way it started with the *News American* editor's concern about drinking among his workers.

The refulgently whiskered Lawrence and his church became, over the years, a resource and a refuge for the poor, the homeless and those with drinking and other substance abuse issues. From time to time, there was an encampment of homeless at the front entrance. Lawrence refused city officials' request that he evict them until some more enterprising occupants started to build sheds.

St. Vincent's fortunes rose and fell. For some years when many in Baltimore moved to the suburbs, the late night Mass "helped keep the parish alive," put enough money in the collection plates on weekends to hold the church's head above water.

In 2013, though, 99 years after it started, Father Lawrence said the final printers' Mass. No more than a dozen or so worshipers were showing up. By then, he managed all the priestly duties: weddings, christenings, funerals and Masses. There was no longer a need to accommodate printers. There were virtually none of them left. The *News American* had gone out of business in 1986, two decades earlier. The *Sun* soldiered on, its workforce reduced by technology, the internet and ruinous speculating by investors with no knowledge of or love for newspapers. The proud printers and compositors and typesetters and linotype operators had been gone from the fourth floor makeup room at the *Sun* for upwards of a decade. Machines had once again sent workingmen into the street.

In better times, St. Vincent's had given pressmen, strippers and beyond-deadline young men a second chance. The Catholic church in its wisdom had provided for Baltimore's newspapermen..

57

And Now?

All three of the papers I worked for are still standing. But barely. All three are weakened.

The 911 terror attack and the spiking cost of Manhattan housing had given Jersey City a deeper tax base and a trendy vibe, a night life with fern bars and firehouse pizza élan. At the same time, the *Jersey Journal* lost its footing literally. Land was more valuable for development – condos and the like – than for a dying newspaper. Da Joisey took itself to Secaucus, miles from Journal Square and the heart of the city it once defined. Arguably still part of Jersey but rudely uprooted, the paper limped away hoping to find a sustainable formula: just like so many other papers once called the backbone of democracy.

It was not the first time change challenged the hometown sheet.

The city and the newspaper were one in 1929 when Mayor Frank Hague tried to re-name Journal Square in honor of the nation's veterans. Surely he wanted to honor them, but he was angry about critical editorials.

The people said "no" to a new name. The city and the newspaper had a visceral alliance underestimated by the willful mayor. The newspaper, marked by 5-foot-high red letters on the building's roof was home ground, resonant, soul stirring, permanent. There were no polls then, but political people have antennae. Hague had expanded the city payroll when it suited him. He had built a hospital open to the poor as well as to those who could pay. He had earned (paid for) a close alliance with the Catholic Church. His influence ended at the newspaper's front door. What a tribute.

That was then.

In 2014, the Joisey management warned its staff the end might be near. But it managed to hang on. I spoke briefly with Margaret Schmidt, one of the paper's editors. I told her I'd started there.

I gave her my *Jersey Journal* dates by way of introduction, 1963-1965. Like many of us, 1963, even without the November 22 date, resonates still.

Of course, she knew of Gene Farrell.

"He was legendary," she said. Schmidt had worked for his wife, Lois — also legendary. Lois had been the first woman in a professional hockey team locker room.

The paper had become a tabloid, hoping to extend its reach. It just celebrated its 150th anniversary. Would I like to see the celebratory magazine? She sent it along. Among many important stories, the most famous was the Page 1 brief announcing that *no one* had been indicted that day. This was news? It was since one pol after another headed for the courthouse, it seemed, every day. Here was New Jersey politics in a paragraph.

Then came the Kushner development company. It bought the building that housed da Joisey's offices. Yes, that Kushner, the President's son-in-law. A Kushner project was to follow at 30 Journal Square, the newspaper's address since the 1920s. A bit of inescapable irony here. Trump has famously called reporters "enemies of the people." I don't know if Jared shares that view. (He had owned a newspaper, the *New York Observer*. That alone does not answer the question.)

Either way, business is business. Had the Kushner company played some role in the Joisey's survival albeit indirect? Did the sale help to finance new life in Secaucus?

Whatever — the red lettered *Jersey Journal* sign was to remain at Journal Square.

Nice touch — even if it makes the Joisey competitive for "Ghost Paper" of the year.

58

The ProJo

Haven Brothers food truck still rolls up next to Providence City Hall on Fulton Street at 5 p.m. sharp. (In 2018, it celebrated its 125th anniversary.) If your constitution is up to it, you can get a hot dog and a coffee-milk (Rhode Island for latte) at 4 in the morning. Not me. I couldn't imagine then what the market might have been for hot dogs at dawn: maybe late or early shift workers, pressmen and stoned Brown and RISD kids.

I found the same old city with some truly grand changes.

The Providence River had been opened to the world. The city had stripped off the river's covering, cleaning it thoroughly, getting rid of the debris and the stench. The river had become an entertainment venue. Something called WaterFire went on there periodically. Gondolas plied the friendly waters of this still majority Italian American city. Fires in braziers along the river – and fireworks – draw thousands.

A few blocks north and west, the railroad station and the railroad itself had been removed and rerouted. An immense urban shopping mall has been inserted somewhat awkwardly on a hill below the magnificent state capitol building with its Independent Man statue on the dome, a tribute to Roger Williams, the state's founder.

The paper's old line Yankee family heirs let go in 1996, selling out before the newspaper market collapsed entirely. They held on longer than they might have, anchored by family ties, and some said, to a thin strand of noblesse oblige and a semblance of control they may once have seen as their birthright.

A bronze plaque on the brick wall to the right of the building's entrance gave the 6-foot high-water mark in the hurricane of 1938. Two hundred fifty people died in the storm, water sluicing into the shallow downtown streets.

I never thought of it when I was working there, but here was an immutable illustration of the newspaper as part of the city's foundation. The *Journal* felt the water rise just as the rest of the city did.

The newspaper was a Providence institution as much as churches and the school system, the business organizations, government and the civic club were institutions. People saw it as their paper. It was as much a part of the city's physical and human fabric as the train station, the shimmering capitol building, the hot dog vendor or the state's unofficial motto, Hope. We were the place to go if you couldn't get a hearing anywhere else.

The *Providence Journal's* first edition appeared on July 23, 1829. For its 100th, a suitable anniversary tribute, I thought, must have been a book. (The *Sun* had celebrated with a strikingly handsome volume written by Mencken and others.)

I checked Google and Amazon. Nothing. I drove to a pair of used book shops in a downtown Providence I hardly recognized. You could get a proper latte or cappuccino in daring new coffee joints

One of the booksellers suggested checking with Paper Nautilus, an upscale competitor on Wayland Square east of the Brown campus. I drove up College Hill past the Rhode Island School of Design, the first Baptist Church in America and the Brown campus.

There it was. Not a book but a newspaper insert, a broad sheet larger than a tire or auto dealer ad. As if to apologize for the absence of a book, the editors pointed out the use of "coated book paper...adapted to permanent preservation." An insert was no doubt less expensive. It certainly spared the delivery boys. If a carrier had 70 customers, he couldn't be expected to heft 70 books.

The Nautilus copy had held up well. The plus-quality paper and light blue color had distinction. Even after 85 years, the document retained a measure of gravitas.

An unnamed reporter or editor wrote the birthday message. It seemed to me no less than a general meditation on any newspaper's role in society. He quoted Lord Morley, a British newspaperman and political leader of the

1880s. I had never heard of him. Suddenly he was speaking to me – and making my argument to myself. History was in us. Even ink-stained wretches had a certain nobility.

"Newspapers, as well as men, are… of the frame and fiber of Antique Time. Old influences of which they themselves are unconscious contribute to their character. Forgotten voices speak through them," Morley wrote.

Every one of us, he said, "has all the centuries in him." Each generation picks up a shard or scrap or vapor of the lives committed to (the newspaper) by the men and (eventually) women who worked there.

My own fiber and frame were one with this long, anonymous phalanx of chroniclers. With my hands on the 100th anniversary tribute, I was suddenly in communication with a *Journal* writer who wrote 85 years earlier about the soul of the paper. And he was writing, of course, about editors and reporters who had done the work 100 years before him.

We were Lord Morley's proof. We were called upon by the ghosts of our newspaper forebears to uphold the standards of care and discipline and integrity. At their best, the *Journal* and other newspapers spoke for their city and state; intervened for those of no means; provided a measure of stability; validated a way of life; established standards of civility; provided new generations of reporters to the bigger league papers. People could learn the vocabulary of issues they were talking about. They'd read it in "the Pro-Jo," "da Joisey" or the *Sun*.

Envisioning a second hundred years, the newspaper's owners took a shot in 1929 at expressing what had guided their paper through its first century.

"We have always regarded the *Journal* as an institution, as well as a property, and for no personal advantage have we overlooked that policy, or sacrificed its reputation to its profits," they said.

In 1929, the *Journal* company's president declared:

"We have in our keeping a fine old institution which is bigger than we are and which we hope will still be flourishing long after we are gone."

I thought the writer nailed it in his valedictory:

"... (The newspaper) is not the mere product of the present hour, but an institution deep-rooted in the generations that have gone. The activities of innumerable minds and hearts of other days are still busy within it. Ancient ideals and loyalties still play their part in its progress. And, though its face is to the future, it cannot forget the vanished past."

The writer must have assumed his newspaper would be as enduring as Brown and RISD, the Independent Man, the Providence River and even coffee milk.

But, he said, there would be change. And so there was.

The canny old *Providence Journal* owners sold their public trust, their institution, in 1996. A Texas-based "media company" paid $1.2 billion for the paper and a TV station. Jones thought he knew what was coming. He bought some *Journal* stock so he could attend shareholder meetings, including a vote to approve a sale. He offered what might be seen as the newsman's post Internet lament. The sale, he said, was simply wrong.

"It is wrong because Rhode Islanders need this newspaper, need the best newspaper that it's possible for journalists to produce. For most of our citizens it is their only link to knowledge needed to sort out their lives in a complex world. The only place they can turn to for justice, for action, for insight and to find humor in an often-sad community."

He liked to remember a telling *Journal* photograph: a farmer with his hand to his nose in the middle of his pepper field. You couldn't sneeze in Rhode Island without a *Journal* reporter or photographer to record it and say God bless you.

Not to worry, the new owner said. Though it spoke of improving investor profits, smarter did not necessarily mean leaner. Maybe not. More money could be invested in the newsroom or in forming a good website. But that was not the rule.

Reporters were fond of mocking born-yesterday efforts: "I fell off the turnip truck at night, but it wasn't last night."

Nevertheless, someone had to be optimistic. Joel Rawson, the paper's top editor, hoping to offset the gloom, said:

"I think we can look forward to a demand for excellence."

Twenty years later, I asked how it had turned out.

Rawson gave me some perspective.

"The *Journal* was never a big paper, but it had big ambitions and let us strive for excellence. We were good because we wanted to be. And Michael Metcalf (then the publisher) was willing to pay the bill.

"The new owners never told us what to do or not to do, but over time they strangled the cash flow... The pressure to produce profit never let up. A key, and to my thinking, wrong, demand from Belo was to invest in on-line, not by reinvesting profit, but by cutting the operating budget of the newspaper while maintaining profit. This resulted in hiring freezes, cutting legal support, news hole reductions...

"In the five years between 1996 and 2001 the *Journal* sent between $30 to $40 million a year to Belo. We never touched it. And we got it back at their sufferance."

It worked pretty much the way Brian Jones thought it would. Ben Bagdikian, a recognized media critic and former *Journal* reporter, raised the specter of deep damage. How could a Texas company, he suggested, maintain or even recognize what drove the paper to maintain high standards? "A nagging Yankee guilt" had been required to do so, he said. What did a Texas company know about Yankee anything?

Jack Monaghan, who printed Lioce's too honest hotel review, stayed for a time under the new regime even knowing the end had come. His budget was cut. The newsroom plague called downsizing gained momentum. The institutional, community commitment moved from newspapering to profit-taking. He was proud of the paper's effort to help the newly jobless, but the calling grew faint. He retired.

59

The *Sun*

I had this joking commentary on the newspaper's fate. You walk out in the morning to get it and you don't have to bend over. It floats up into your hand.

The paper had lost weight. To save on the cost of newsprint, it had been trimmed almost to the size of a magazine. It became a house organ for the Orioles and the Ravens, the baseball and football teams. People started cancelling their subscriptions. The hometown newspaper was dying before our eyes.

Maybe. But reporters and editors pushed back.

In 2016, we reminded our colleagues and former readers that we had placed second in the 2016 Pulitzer Prize contest for work during the Freddie Gray calamity.

That event, resulting in brutality charges against city police, led to an alarming spike in the already-high murder rate. A series of police commissioners, including one who had failed to pay income taxes for four years, had to be replaced.

A special squad of gun enforcement officers were convicted of stealing from citizens they'd sworn to serve and protect. With Baltimore seeming to be at the mercy of rogue cops, then Mayor Catherine Pugh said she was busy with other important things and not paying attention to a series of riveting trials. One of her advisers said she had mis-spoken.

Against the backdrop of Freddie Gray, the city seemed to be in free fall.

In the spring of 2019, the *New York Times* commissioned a freelance reporter to write a profile of Baltimore, a once-great American city, imploding. Why hadn't The *Sun* attempted such an assessment? Why indeed. Such a project, done right, would have demanded resources. The right perspective, moreover, can be difficult when you are immersed in a daily struggle to survive – when you are a major part of the story.

But there was some good news. The slimmed down newspaper was still on its feet. Canzian was back after two years teaching in the city's public schools. Reporters waged a campaign to get her re-hired. It was about her skills, but I think it also had something to do with having an organized mind in the midst of chaos in and out of the newsroom.

The managing editor, Triffon Alatzas, illustrated some of the same steadying force. He had worked productively with one of the previous publishers to avoid deeper staff cuts reductions and even to add talent – reporters with an investigative bent. Papers in general had been so starved of reporters that real investigations – more than a phone call – was unaffordable. Alatzas, himself, illustrated the new world of newspapers: he became publisher as well as executive editor – two big jobs rolled into one.

Following other papers, the *Sun* left Calvert Street near city center, moving to its printing operation in Port Covington south of the city. It needed a more efficient facility, leaders explained, wired for the new world of technology. The new digs looked like a small airline hanger, a pristine, well-lighted place outfitted by every iteration of computer screen. Some device or other kept track of what stories were trending."

Hyper conscious of the new reality, the newspaper installed new protective/ safety devices – bullet-proof glass and tightened border security. Getting into and out of the newsroom required various door locking and unlocking protocols.

The move from Calvert Street came at some expense, to be sure. The unseen aura of the place, the markers of human habitation and endeavor stayed behind to be further eliminated by whatever replaced decades of chronicling the life of a city.

There would be nothing like Jim Keat's never-washed coffee cup. No rows of smoked-out cigarette butts standing on their filter ends or leaving burn marks on a desk. No "ego row" where reporters of high self-regard chatted and preened. There would be nothing to identify the territory commanded by "Brownie," copy kid for life, gofer and dictation-taker. (almost) as essential as Ettlin. Surely there was no spike, but those had been gone from the Calvert Street newsroom. Nothing remained but the echoing emptiness.

The old symbolic importance of a downtown newspaper location was gone, swept away in Baltimore by, among other things, two or three new potential center cities.

The new city room, I thought, was everything management claimed. More efficient undoubtedly. No wasted space.

Of course, you can't take the intangibles with you – or even the tangibles: the famous Mencken valedictory was gone. His famous exit line had been painted on the back lobby wall behind the first floor receptionist. Looking back on a mis-spent life, he had said, he was pretty sure newspaper reporting was the best life had to offer, the life of kings, he said. Even better, I thought. Unlike kings, you didn't have to raise an army or have anyone killed.

So what would be next? More of the same with fewer hands to handle it. In 2019, a series of challenging "big stories" tested a beleaguered city room. (Could the city itself prosper and survive if there were no newspaper, no *Sun*?)

• A woman was reportedly stabbed to death while trying to help one of the city's many panhandlers. Another blow to a city already competing for murder capital of the nation. But wait. The woman had been killed by her husband and his daughter in pursuit of her life insurance. They attempted to outrun police who had quickly uncovered the scam. The cops did their jobs. The *Sun* did its.

• A financial crisis at the city's renowned symphony orchestra demanded close attention. To do the complete job of newspapering, every element of city life had to be covered. Many readers cared deeply about the symphony at a time when music seemed an essential anchor of a city losing its grasp of civilized, city life. The newspaper's talented, long time arts writer retired and was not replaced. Coverage would be handled by already ever-taxed reporters. Next man or woman up.

• And then, the mayor and eight other members of the University of

Maryland Medical System's volunteer board of directors were caught – by the *Sun* – in systematic self-dealing. Mayor Pugh had sold the board $500,000 worth of books she self-published. Were the books a fig leaf covering payoffs? The quality of the "books," the half million dollars involved and the aura of a "volunteer" board members dipping into the public till came to light via the *Sun*.

• State and federal investigations began. Had Pugh paid taxes on this unprecedented income flow? Under intense pressure, she resigned. The *Sun* had changed the face of Baltimore.

• All of this made two critically important points. The *Sun* had not become a "ghost," one of those papers hollowed out by staff cuts and the greed of new owners. The importance of a newspaper could not have been more clearly demonstrated. The *Sun* did what newspapers do. At the same time, it showed what might happen when there is no newspaper.

The question now? How long can the paper operate at this level? Many in Baltimore, to be sure, believe it has succumbed already to layoffs and downsizing.

Not yet.

The question now: How long can the newspaper operate at this level? With sufficient staff, the answer would be indefinitely. Pride, energy, professionalism and the calling will sustain.

But only up to a point. *Sun* reporters were offered no pay increase – for the 7th year in a row. Medical insurance coverage was cut. Workers were asked to pay $75 a week to park on the company lot.

Job searches inevitably underway already will accelerate. Talented, committed journalists will follow the *Sun's* chief editorial writer Andy Green out the door. A talented writer/thinker/manager, he will be vice president for communications at Johns Hopkins University.

Not everyone will be so favored. But others at the *Sun* – and at newspapers across the nation – are likely to leave the defense of democracy. The exodus is well underway.

60

A Grace Note

Old Sunners contributed to a book on the glory days of the *Sun*. We called it *The Life of Kings*, H.L. Mencken's tribute. The book attracted some attention, but also managed to infuriate those who were:

A) not involved in the project or

B) still working for the paper or

C) sniping at oversights they insisted would never have happened on their watch.

Once a year in the spring, *Sun* layoff casualties, retirees and others convened at the elegant Engineers Club Mount Vernon just up the hill from the *Sun's* old haunt. It's a what-are-you-up-to session with a little bit of show and tell thrown in.

I thought attendance was a bit down in 2018. Time thinned the ranks as relentlessly as downsizing.

We found ways to survive. Reporters are generalists. Many found specialty writing jobs. Others found work outside the business. We subsisted on memories and news of the odd book sale by our brothers and sisters.

My State House colleague, John Frece, arrived with his just-released biography of former U.S. Senator Joe Tydings of Maryland. Tom Linthicum's book about an Episcopal bishop was to be released at an assembly in Dallas. Antero Pietila had finished a tome on the legacy of Johns Hopkins, the man, and his not always uplifting legacy. And we expect new mysteries from Dan Fesperman and Laura Lippman.

Book-in-hand or not, old names and faces and remembered stories prompted smiles and conversations.

Copy editor extraordinaire, Jeff Landau, was there, uncovering in my odd collection of city room keepsakes a story about Tracy Rozhan, a fine writer with the reporter's reflex concern about an editor's touch or lack thereof.

She had gone up to Landau one evening with an appeal for care in whatever he was about to do with her story.

"Be graceful," she implored.

"Like Swan Lake," he promised.

61

Cigar Box

He wrote thousands of columns, editorials, profiles and news articles. He made himself a shaper of public policy. His judgment elected leaders. He won a Pulitzer Prize. When he died, his newspaper reprised his life on Page One.

Eulogies flowed from family and friends and public officials. What a glorious career, what a valuable life. We liked to give our own "a good send-off."

And yet, thinking back, something was missing. What did *he* think of his life, his influence, his place in the community? Surely, he would have avoided dilating on his Constitutional responsibilities. So, wouldn't his recollections have been important to share? No one could remember such an effort.

And then, an odd discovery, a cache of clips. A friend, helping to dispose of his books and papers and plaques and faded convention credentials, found a handful of rubber-banded stories in a cigar box. A secret last will and testament?

The story made the rounds, with no detail, no characterization. What sort of stories had been in the box? The friend could not be found. The box might as well have remained a secret.

Maybe it was no big deal. Maybe they were simply stories he wouldn't have been embarrassed to have someone find and read. Maybe there was no lesson. Or maybe it was another show of the grizzled newsman's discounting of his work.

The somewhat mysterious story came back to me occasionally. I had my own collection of favorites. I like to think every story I wrote had a purpose and a place in my pantheon. Some, I am sure, don't measure up. No matter.

I always had a second chance. Journalism was a demanding enterprise, but there was always tomorrow.

When I was a student at the University of North Carolina, I often walked from my dormitory, through a grass and weed covered cemetery, on the way to the track and field locker room. (I threw the discus. I won the Atlantic Coast Conference Championship in 1960. Not to date myself at all.)

A headstone there has come to mind often:

"He fails and he alone who hath not striven." (I wonder what wise, amazing human story lay buried there.) I can't subscribe completely to the forgiving inscription, but I think of it now and then. Maybe it's a fallback against the reality of occasional, inevitable failure.

As for the great man's cigar box legacy, I was happy to find more work that pleased me. Like Mrs. Verdiramo, a grateful mother who took a wreath around her parish on All Saints Day in honor of her pledge to God if only her son might survive. Her son told the obituary writer in Jersey City that she had one wish for her life. She wanted to die on All Saints Day and she did. It was no panic-driven, easy to forget promise. I learned a lesson from her. Some people kept their promises even if no one would ever know if they did or not.

There were other stories like hers "out there" and I would find them.

I hope I met Stocker's high standards. Elliott, you will remember, helped me become a better judge of my own work.

A former city editor and conscience of the paper, he demanded to see the goods we (he and I) promised. If we ran a column called "In Perspective," he wanted to see some perspective. He was going to demand it. So was I, after he showed me my responsibility.

I realize now he was my grumpy, demanding muse. (He would have scoffed at the airs of a college kid. "Don't wait for a muse. Just do the damn work.") But, after watching and listening to him, I wanted all my stories to have a shape and sense of purpose, gotten into the paper with fidelity. Or what was a newspaper for? I wanted to offer a glimpse of how we lived in our day. Stories of this kind were not always seen as fundamental newspaper fare, but they were. They were stories that move us a step beyond, stories that got a little closer to who we idiosyncratic humans are. To me, those stories were the soul of our work. They showed us striving, speaking out for justice and, if finding no audience – failing, in fact – one might soldier on expecting a different outcome. "Success," Churchill said, "was stumbling from one failure to the next with no loss of enthusiasm."

My cigar box, if I leave one, will have stories like that and more personal ones: the perfect snow-garlanded Christmas tree, cut and strapped to the roof of the van; the ornaments carefully labeled as to time and gift-giver; how my twins and I would live after the death of the Muppets genius Jim Henson – how Kermit and Big Bird and Ernie could go on without him. How we might survive.

There would be room for a story about Baltimore through the eyes of visiting writers; a color story on the 1983 World Champion Orioles. (Who had decided I could be sent on such an important story? I found it reassuring, some evidence that colleagues thought I could handle it. Would I ever get beyond the need for that kind of validation? Probably not.) I saw myself cheering for the woman, the hero, the brave soul who found her way out of addiction in a third-chance program.

It was always personal. The Thanksgiving with my son's family in Louisiana; a home repair job with an epic universality of a headline: "Hanging on 'Til Help Arrives." There was a Jules Verne-like drawing to go with it, a man floundering through the depths, finding no traction on an underwater bike. My stories about the junk man Sam Corrado.

How privileged was I? Immensely. I could write about my life and suggest it might represent the lives of others. It was, I fear, an under-appreciated gift of newspapers. Others had the same or similar experiences, but I got to write them – if only I could find perspective and sometimes a picture.

"He fails and he alone who hath not striven."

If my cigar box involved second guessing, I might have wondered why I didn't bypass the (instantly fading) glory of government political writing for these "people" stories. I couldn't go far with that lament, because I know why. Politics was the star-strewn path. I knew we had to show lawmakers working like Speaker Mike Busch to get it right – important because they were so often held in low regard. I think that part of the job was undervalued, the part that gave readers/voters confidence in government – just as important as the unmasking of corruption. You had to find human perspective in these stories as well.

And there was my profile of Claiborne Pell. Had we let the jokes obscure the man's humanity, something voters saw and JFK missed. Claiborne Pell, a rich man threading the needle, an innocent, a striver who changed our world.

And there were two more dimensions to my story. I spent a decade doing stories and commentary for Baltimore's National Public Radio affiliate. With my nagging partner, Sunni Khalid, I did a series on the election of Maryland governors; a series of stories about the Baltimore Symphony's Orch-kids Program, and reports from the 2008 and 2012 Presidential nominating conventions. Over that same decade, I wrote a weekly column for the *Daily Record*. These pieces were read by 6,000 of Baltimore's most discerning lawyers and businessmen. I thank them all for the privilege.

62

Ring the Bells

Ring the bells that still can ring.
Forget your perfect offering
There is a crack in everything
That's how the light gets in.

Leonard Cohen

Newspapers found the cracks. What will replace them? Social media? Blogs? Will the survivors be honestly and independently committed to the light? Who will pay some freelance to do a story a paper didn't have to have? Will newspaper standards live on with the new "platforms."?

Standards and objectives are what matter. Not the medium, not ink on paper, not digits or whatever.

The *Sun,* had a splendid motto: "Light for All." We were proud of it, determined to make it so. (We half-joked about our employer's way of achieving light – holding down our paychecks.)

Mildly cynical jokes became part of the reporter and editor mantra. We were there to shine the light: that responsibility made up for the meager pay. We accepted a calling. To be one of the small batteries in the spotlight of democracy was an honor. (This is what Russell Baker called dilating on your Constitutional responsibilities. Guilty as charged.)

And now we watch a self-sustaining profession turn to dust.

The losses matter.

The reformer Robert W. McChesney says brave new newspaper claims of undiminished ardor – or unsustainable, herculean effort – offer nothing like an adequate response. "A collection of niche Websites covering different aspects of a community are well and good, but even in combination they cannot recreate the coherence and unity of a well-edited, resourced and respected newspaper ..."

The question: how do we maintain quality journalism in a world driven more by profit than by calling or by the demands of democracy? Has it ever been thus? More than we knew.

Democracy surely will die in darkness, as the *Washington Post* observes. Fewer papers mean less light. Surveys show people think newspapers are just fine. A commentary we try to ignore.

When the paper was the only game in town, when wealthy owners ran papers as a public service, these life and death questions did not arise (for the most part).

They must arise now. Newspaper standards are a model, a template, a guidepost. They are indispensable. They will save us from many evils, including the devious "fake news" label hung on real, embarrassing or even criminal news.

The Constitution and the First Amendment call on us – always – to act with the passion and concern of those who made us free. (I know, more dilating.)

At the time of the revolution, a European visitor observed, many Americans read the Bible. On the other hand, he said, everyone read newspapers.

Jefferson and Washington and Madison were political leaders with faith in the people's ability to learn and act appropriately on the news they got from the papers – the number of which, with their aggressive assistance, doubled and tripled in the first years of the republic.

Madison said: "A people who mean to be their own governors must arm themselves with the power which knowledge gives. A popular government without popular information or the means of acquiring it is but a prologue to farce or tragedy or perhaps both."

Jefferson more famously said: "Were it left to me to decide whether we should have government without newspapers or newspapers without a government, I should not hesitate for a moment to prefer the latter."

I take him to have meant that you could always have government but maybe not such a good one without newspapers. And if you didn't have newspapers it would be vastly more difficult to achieve change.

Less often quoted but equally important, in the next sentence, Mr. Jefferson said, "I should mean that every man should receive those (newspapers) and be capable of reading them."

He made clear his pledge: "To preserve the freedom of the human mind and freedom of the press, every spirit should be ready to devote itself to martyrdom." Once again, it's not the medium, it's the standards – the calling, even.

This, I assume, is why the Yale philosopher and political scientist Timothy Snyder wrote his powerful little book, *On Tyranny:*

"Institutions cannot defend themselves," he said. "We have to.

"It is institutions that help us preserve democracy... They fall one after the other unless each is defended from the beginning. So, choose an institution you care about – the courts, a newspaper, a law, a labor union, a federal agency – and take its side."

We must see ourselves the way Washington, Jefferson and Madison saw themselves: outnumbered but unwilling to serve a king or tyrant.

Ring the bells.

Acknowledgments

I am grateful to a half-century of colleagues. Names are the first to go, of course, so with apologies I offer these as representative: Elliott Stocker for demanding perspective; John Lanclottie for assuring me I'd be working with the "cleanest" people if I stayed in the business; Joe Ungaro who loved newspapers as much as any of us; Martha who jumped with me into public housing as if it were a good idea; Miriam Satterfield, whose laugh I can hear and smile I can see today; Buddy George who chaperoned me in the understandably curious black community of Providence; Mike Nalbandian, the Galoise smoking eminence grise of the poverty war; Zorzi, Eileen; Mom (aka Wooton), Frece, Watson, Luxenberg; Brownie; the polymath, Andy Green; Suzanna Craine, Tracy Miller and my partner and indispensable teammate, Carole Hamlin, who held life together; my memoir team: Margaret, Fred, and Hattie; and for the skilled Otter Bay group: Ann, Cherie, and Kate, and for Dave Goldsmith, a man for all glitches, on-call for life.

I have done my best to evict the Gremlins, of which I am the leader. I am grateful for the many insights and "good grabs" (found errors). Ziner, Winternitz, Dawn Raffel, the best; Charles Salsberg, for many favors and Patty Dan. I sincerely regret the unfound others.